UNCOMMON ENDURANCE

12 Women's Stories of Resilience and Redemption

Presented by

TAMARA STEELE & TRACYE BURR

ELOHAI
INTERNATIONAL
PUBLISHING & MEDIA

Print ISBN: 978-1-953535-84-9
E-book ISBN: 978-1-953535-90-0

Published by ELOHAI International Publishing & Media
P.O. Box 1883
Cypress, TX 77410
hello@elohaiintl.com
elohaiintl.com

Printed in the United States of America

Dedication and Acknowledgements

The authors of this anthology project collectively dedicate *Uncommon Endurance* to every woman who has ever felt overwhelmed by life's circumstances. To all the women who doubted their strength and ability to endure life's challenges, we hope this book brings you courage, inspiration, and freedom to feel and love again.

We also would like to thank ELOHAI International Publishing & Media's Publisher, Natasha Watson, for her guidance, encouragement, and expertise during the entire project.

Finally, our anthology project would not be complete without acknowledging our loved ones for their unwavering love, support, and patience throughout this project. We acknowledge our ancestors who paved the way for us to tell our story and from whom we all draw strength, wisdom, and courage to tell our stories with a spirit of excellence.

Contents

CHAPTER 1

Burned but Not Consumed: Beauty for Ashes

by Tamara Steele

My mind races with so many thoughts and experiences that shape who I am today and influence how I've struggled to become the woman I am. Let me take you down memory lane and paint a picture for you.

The earliest memory I can recall is from the age of four. I loved visiting my maternal grandmother and playing with my seven-year-old sister and cousins.

My grandmother had a big home—five bedrooms, three baths, a living room, a dining room, and a family room. It was a place full of warmth and laughter, the perfect sanctuary for childhood games and imagination. We played hide-and-seek, dress-up, and anything else our imaginations could create. One day, I decided to play dress-up and discovered my grandmother's perfume. I vividly remember wearing a yellow turtleneck dress with long sleeves, feeling fancy and grown-up.

As a four-year-old, I had no sense of moderation. I sprayed the perfume liberally onto my dress, saturating the neck and chest area.

The aroma was overwhelming. My sister came into the room and caught the powerful scent. That's when she had what seemed like a brilliant idea: to kill the smell using a match.

The idea wasn't as random as it sounds. Our grandparents often burned matches to eliminate strong odors in the bathroom, and my sister thought the same logic could work here. She figured all she needed to do was light a match near my neck, and the overpowering smell would disappear.

Unbeknownst to either of us, perfume is highly flammable. The moment the match came close, I went up in flames. I can still hear my screams—raw and piercing. My sister panicked and ran to the bathroom, desperately trying to turn on the water to extinguish the fire. But she was too small to reach the faucet. Frantic, she ran downstairs to get our grandmother.

Meanwhile, I instinctively ran to the nearest bedroom—my great-grandmother's room, at the top of the stairs. I vividly remember the terror in her eyes when she saw me engulfed in flames. My great-grandmother, who was paralyzed, fell from her chair, and tried to crawl toward me. She never made it to me, but her effort left a lasting imprint on my mind and heart.

My grandmother then appeared, running up the stairs with her house shoes flying off. She threw herself at me and smothered the flames on my neck and chest with her bare hands. I remember her praying aloud, calling out "Lord Jesus" repeatedly. Her faith-filled words became a soothing presence in the chaos. Despite the pain she must have felt, she didn't stop until the flames were out.

Shortly after, my mother's cousin arrived to comfort me until the ambulance came. I was in shock, the pain feeling surreal. My grandmother had to pick her mother off the floor and ensure she was okay. I remember her strength and composure despite the chaos.

Before the ambulance arrived, my mother ran into the house, frantic and terrified. She rode with me in the ambulance, her presence bringing me a fragile sense of calm. I was first taken to Kaiser Permanente and later transferred to Children's Hospital, where doctors moved quickly to treat the third-degree burns on my neck and chest—the most severe kind.

These burns destroyed the skin's top layer (epidermis) and the middle layer (dermis), along with some nerve endings. The doctors worried I might lose mobility in my neck or sensation in the affected areas.

I spent over a month in the hospital, too young to grasp the long-term impact this accident would have on my life.

The surgeons performed a skin graft, taking healthy skin from my upper left leg and transplanting it to my burned neck. They couldn't cover the entire area because I was so small. They were careful not to restrict my neck's mobility. When I was discharged, I had to wear a custom-molded neck brace made from plaster. This brace became my shield from the world, a security blanket that hid my scars and protected me from stares, questions, and judgment.

My sister, though just a child, felt immense guilt about what had happened. As we grew older, she shared how deeply it affected her. Yet neither of us could have understood the long-term emotional and physical toll it would take on me.

Kindergarten was especially hard. When the doctors finally said I could take off the brace, I felt exposed. Without it, I faced stares, whispers, and taunts. I learned how cruel children could be. Some didn't want to play with me; others teased me relentlessly.

I convinced myself I wasn't invited to birthday parties or playdates because of my appearance. My mother tried to fill my life with joy, enrolling me in extracurricular activities, but my self-consciousness held me back. Even during swim lessons, I spent more time hiding in the locker room than in the pool, terrified of being seen.

As I grew older, I became skilled at masking my pain. I projected confidence I didn't feel, desperate to fit in and avoid attention. Every time I explained what happened, I relived the trauma. By the time I was fifteen, I begged my mother for another surgery, hoping it would "fix" me and make me look "normal." I wanted so badly to be accepted and to escape the stares and whispers.

After weighing the pros and cons, I opted to have the surgery. I was sure that my life would change for the better. I would "fit in" with the other girls at my high school and receive the acceptance I longed for. I wanted to attend parties and outings without needing to hide my scars. I did not want to avoid school events and other gatherings because I dreaded the negative attention.

My deep memories of being teased at various social outings caused me to avoid attending events. It's like my mind would play the old recording of hurtful incidents over and over. I remember when a high school boy started screaming at the top of his lungs, "Look at this girl; her neck is 'F@%KED up.'" He kept repeating it to get others to stop what they were doing to look at me.

I remember this incident like it was yesterday. I wanted to instantly disappear. I would walk faster, short of running, to remove myself from his presence. Another incident involved my girlfriend's friend. She made very hurtful comments about my (in)ability to attract young men because of my scar. The comments from my peers fed my insecurity.

My decision to undergo the surgery was a leap of faith, a belief that it was my only chance for a better life. The initial signs were promising-the scars were smoother, and I started to envision a new life. But this hope was short-lived. My body began to reject the graft, causing the skin to shrivel and leaving behind new scars. This rejection had a profound impact on my daily life, making my return to school a nightmare.

Classmates who had anticipated a "transformation" now stared at me with curiosity or pity. How could I explain that my hope had turned into another source of pain?

I spent much of my teenage years grappling with low self-worth. I believed my appearance defined me, pouring energy into fashion and makeup to hide my insecurities. My father once told me, "Until you start thinking and feeling good about yourself, nobody else will." His words stuck with me, even as I continued seeking validation from others, especially the boys I dated.

It wasn't until I turned to God that I began to heal. Through prayer, I sought answers about my worth and purpose. God revealed that my scars were not a punishment but a testament to resilience—a way to connect with others who carried invisible wounds. He showed me that my pain wasn't just about me; it was part of His plan to help others.

I started to see my scars differently. They no longer defined me— they empowered me. My purpose became clear: to inspire young women and girls to find their worth beyond appearances. My scars are not just a testament to strength, faith, and self-love, but a beautiful reflection of these qualities.

Embracing vulnerability, I found the courage to say, "I will trust you, God, even when I don't have all the answers. I will trust you even when

I don't feel like depending on you." This vulnerability is not a weakness, but a beautiful strength that we all possess.

Even when doubt, fear, and worry knock at my mind's door, I make a conscious choice to trust. I trust that you, God, know what is best for me, and I release my attachment to the outcome of my life. This act of trust is a total surrender and a powerful decision that I make with every fiber of my being - knowing that when I let go of the desire to control my life, I demonstrate my faith in you.

I took to heart Jesus's statement to the Centurion, "Go; it shall be done for you as you have believed" (Matthew 8:13 NASB), and I reminded myself of my father's words, "If you don't think you look good, nobody else will." I refused to listen to those who made me feel bad about my appearance. My scar would no longer define my worth and beauty. I realized that I could be set FREE by believing God defined who I was and that I was more than enough despite my scar. This understanding of the power of belief in shaping my identity inspired me, as I recognized that my power was in who I chose to believe, God vs. others.

Reflections on Resilience:

Life has a way of refining us, not unlike how fire purifies gold. The scars we carry—visible or invisible—may feel like permanent reminders of pain, but they can also serve as evidence of survival, strength, and transformation. My journey taught me that what the world sees as broken, God sees as an opportunity to create something new, something extraordinary.

In the Bible, Isaiah 61:3 speaks of God giving us "beauty for ashes." This promise doesn't erase the fire we've endured but redefines its purpose. The fire that threatened to destroy us can instead refine us, leaving behind a beauty born of resilience, courage, and faith.

We all face moments that threaten to consume us—moments of loss, heartbreak, rejection, or pain. But the truth is, with God, we are never consumed. Instead, He uses those experiences to transform us and prepare us for the purpose He has set before us. What I once saw as a source of pain has become my testimony. My scars are no longer a symbol of what was lost but a declaration of what was gained: wisdom, empathy, and strength.

I encourage you to look at your own life through this lens. What are the ashes in your story? What moments felt like they would destroy you but instead shaped you into who you are today? Trust that God's promises hold true. He will take what was meant for harm and turn it for good. He will exchange your ashes for beauty, your mourning for joy, and your despair for hope.

The fire may have burned me, but it did not consume me. With God's grace, I turned my pain into purpose and my scars into symbols of victory. So, I invite you to embrace your own story, scars and all, and trust that God can transform your ashes into something beautiful.

As the visionary Founder and CEO of EVOLVE, a Global Women's Collaborative Community, **TAMARA STEELE** embodies the spirit of empowerment, unity, and transformative leadership. Her dedication to fostering a world where women support, uplift, and inspire one another is truly remarkable. Under her leadership, EVOLVE has empowered countless women to reach their full potential, fostering a global community of unwavering support.

Tamara's illustrious career spans over 30 years, during which she has worn multiple hats with grace and excellence. She has excelled in each role, from being a certified executive coach and lifestyle strategist to an author, speaker, attorney at law, and former administrative law judge. Her insights into personal and professional development have charted new territories in women's empowerment and leadership, inspiring others with her remarkable versatility and adaptability.

Moreover, Tamara's spiritual depth as a licensed minister and ordained pastor adds a unique dimension to her work, blending spiritual principles with actionable life strategies. This unique blend has been instrumental in her work at EVOLVE, where she has led workshops and retreats that focus on holistic personal development. Her former roles as Deputy County Counsel for the Alameda and Monterey County Counsel Offices and as Administrative Law Judge for the State of California are further testaments to her exemplary integrity, wisdom, and leadership.

Tamara is a source of inspiration and encouragement to many women who cross paths with her. Her work as the founder and host of the Do You Retreat, a health and wellness retreat designed to empower and equip women to live purpose-driven lives with clarity, ease, and sustainability, speaks to her commitment to uplifting others. The retreat, held annually in various locations, offers a range of breakout sessions and activities focused on personal and professional development. She recently launched Tamara Steele Ministries, hosting an event entitled 'Women at the Well,' – a full-day event where women received wellness for their souls through spiritual teachings, faith-centered breakout sessions, prayer, worship, and self-reflection.

Tamara's academic journey is a testament to her dedication to learning. She received her Juris Doctorate from the University of California San Francisco Law School (formerly U.C. Hastings College of the Law) and her Bachelor of Science in Business Administration from the University of San Francisco. She also received her Bachelor of Arts in Biblical Studies from Northern California Bible College (Co-Valedictorian), her ministerial license and ordination as a pastor from the Jezreel School of Theology (Honors), and her executive/ life coach certification from the Institute for Professional Excellence in Coaching (IPEC).

Tamara can be reached at tamarasteele.com and/or tamarasteele.org.

CHAPTER 2

Ascending Beyond Childhood Trauma

by Toni Rochelle

When I was eight years old, my Big Mama's sister, who is my great aunt, told me to pack a bag, get dressed, and be ready in fifteen minutes. I was juiced! That meant we were going to ride the city bus, either the number fifteen or the thirty-two. It was going to be a good day because we were either going to the welfare office, a doctor's appointment, or the grocery store. Those were the only places we ever went.

We stepped on the bus and it was just me and my auntie. Now I knew better than to ask questions because back then, you did what you were told. We couldn't ask a thousand questions like kids do today. We would get our butts whooped, or slapped, or a big object thrown at us. My auntie never had a problem throwing whatever was next to her at our heads when she wanted to express to us that she was not happy. I knew how to pick my battles.

I sat and enjoyed myself, looking at people entering and exiting the bus, and staring out of the window. I imagined that we were going on a trip or somewhere exciting, a place I had never heard of before. I was excited at that very moment, enjoying the scenery and simply imagining my life with full abundance and happiness. However, I did have this nagging feeling. I couldn't help but think about my brother. Why didn't he come? Where was he? I missed him and I could not wait to rub it in his face that I went out with my great aunt and he didn't. Suddenly, the ring from the string on the bus alerted me that it was time to get off. I was still sitting and daydreaming when I heard my auntie say, "Toni girl, come on."

We ended up on the east side of Oklahoma City on North Martin Luther King Jr. Avenue. We walked into a neighborhood full of brick houses that all looked the same. It was *The Hood*. This was a hot day and there were tons of kids playing outside.

We approached a house with a metal fence. My auntie knocked on the screen door a couple of times. A toothless older woman approached the door with Jheri Curl juice dripping down her neck. The lady invited us in, took my bag, and handed me a big cup of red Kool-Aid. She then asked me if I wanted to go outside to play with the other kids. I said yes.

I went outside and was having a good old time. It was like I had known these kids forever. We were just about to play Hide-and-Seek and I had to use the bathroom. I went into the house and asked where it was, and when I came out of the bathroom, I asked where my auntie went, and the lady with no teeth told me "she left." My eyes grew big and my heart started pounding super-fast. Why would she leave me? I felt like I had done something wrong that I would get a whooping for.

Now I didn't know this lady well at all, so I began to ask, "When will she be back?"

"Never." She had an attitude.

"Why did she leave me here?"

"I am your grandmother."

"Wait, what? No you're not. You're not my mom's mother."

She said, "No I'm not. I'm your dad's mother."

Wait, what?

"You're going to be living here with me and your two cousins.

I was confused. *What cousins? My dad's mother? Wait a minute. This doesn't make any sense,* I thought. I had never met my father nor did I know his name. Why would my auntie just leave me here and not say goodbye? I was mad, sad, and very much confused. I asked if I could call my auntie, but realized I didn't even know the number, and our phone had been cut off for a while. So what was I supposed to do?

As I was caught in my thoughts, a dark-skinned man with big, scary hazel eyes, who looked as if he was full of sneaky thoughts, approached me. I hated the way he looked at me. It was like he was ready to make a move—like a dog in heat. He was tall, but he didn't walk in a room like a confident man. Instead, he was a thug. He was dirty looking and I hated the way he walked—as if he was untouchable... you know, like he was God's gift to the world or something. He smelled like sex! Back then, of course I didn't know that smell, but I remember him smelling 'stanky.' Later, I would find out that he always smelled like sex.

When he was not taking advantage of me in private, do you know he would joke with me on a regular basis as if we were the best of cousins?!

It had not even been twenty-four hours after my auntie left me with these people that I went from getting physically abused, by her, to now encountering my perverted cousin, Mr. Hazel Eyes, with his long fingers and Freddy Krueger nails. That was not better. He seemed kind of slow when I first met him. His eyes looked crossed and his head look like a peanut. Whenever he said something to me, I felt this black cloud hovered over me. Just then, my toothless grandmother announced she was going to play BINGO, as if this day could not get any worse.

"Go ahead, Grandma and make sure you win. Oh, and I will watch Toni," replied Mr. Hazel Eyes.

Mind you, I didn't know him like that. Hell, I didn't know her like that. I guess my grandmother didn't care about my comfort at that moment. Apparently nobody cared about me that day, or at all. That was the first day my innocence was stripped from me. I didn't even know what that meant, but I knew it was not right. I knew that it didn't feel right physically or mentally. It hurt like it didn't belong in me. I remember digging my fingernails so deep in his skin that he bled. Who would've thought my day would have turned out like this? At this point, I was actually thinking about killing myself. My childhood had been stripped from me within seconds. He was such a punk!

Looking back, I can remember how scared I was when he showed me his gun. That action made it clear that I did not run anything and he was in complete control. That was the first day I saw a gun. That was the first day I felt a gun inside of me. That was the first day a man's lips touched my body. Some would call it their first kiss. That was the day that I was given away to my mother's ex-boyfriend's family—the family of my father who I had never met.

As I processed it all, I thought, wait a minute! Why did my auntie drop me off like I was a piece of trash? I couldn't put two and two together. However, I remember the day before, I asked her about my father. Who was he? Where was he? My auntie never answered me, so I didn't think about it anymore. If I would have known twenty-four hours earlier that I was going to be dropped off like a bag of garbage to people I had never met or even heard of, I promise I would never have asked my auntie anything about my father. At this moment, I felt like I was in a movie—a cruel, surreal plot unfolding because I dared to wonder about my father.

One day we were outside playing as kids did in the '90s. It was a very humid day. Kids were engaged in all sorts of activities: bike riding, jumping rope, just chilling, girls playing with Barbie dolls, and boys playing dodge ball and kick ball. All we wanted was some candy, a pickle, or something cold to drink. Now that may not seem like it would be hard to get, but when you grow up in the projects, things were just not that easy. People who didn't actually grow up in the projects would never understand that those things were considered luxuries.

Our joys came on the first and the fifteenth of the month. Why? Because that's when the food stamps and the money would arrive. Those were the days when we had paper food stamps that were different colors. If I remember correctly, the brown stamps were worth one dollar, green was five dollars, and purple was twenty dollars. Those multicolor blessings came in a booklet twice a month, and my auntie would send us to the store to get her Cheetos, a Dr. Pepper, and Newport Cigarettes. That is when we all would get happy and have something to look forward to.

I was always a different kind of kid. I daydreamed often and talked to my imaginary friend about all my dreams. My dreams were not outrageous; it was not that I wanted a million dollars. I didn't dream of being rich. My mom was addicted to drugs, alcohol, and street life. She was always in and out of jail. I can truly say that me, my mom, and her five kids, have never been in the same room at the same time. We don't even have a family picture with all six of us together. I never met my father nor do I know his name or what nationality he is. To this day I still don't know what he looks like. My dream has always been to have the opportunity to be in the same room with all of us together—me, my brothers, my mother, and my father—all at the same time. I would feel complete. I know that it's just a wish, but it's something to look forward to and I always believed that it actually could happen. I know it's a fairy tale dream but that's all I had.

My oldest brother and I had to live with my great aunt because Big Mama already had so many of her other grandchildren living with her, and nobody else wanted us, or me. My auntie (my mom's aunt) was a really mean lady and she hated me the most. At least that's how she made me feel. If she was not beating us, she would make me and my brother fight each other, and I would try to kill him because I was so mad at her. I would take my anger out on him by beating him up. David and I are a year and a half apart. Do you know she would laugh! She was entertained by it. Other times if she was not up to beating us, she would give us a choice: "Do you want your ass beat or do you want me to attack those hands?" (*That meant she would hit us with a wooden spoon on our hands*). Either way it was a bad and unhealthy way to discipline children. I still don't know why my auntie treated me this way, but I give her grace, now as an adult.

Later on in life, as an adult, I learned why my grandmother didn't take me in. I found out that my mother was getting molested by her stepfather... my grandfather, who is my grandmother's husband. My grandmother actually walked in on my mother getting molested by her stepfather. My grandmother chose to stay with her husband instead of defending her oldest daughter. This crushed my mother and broke her heart. It drove her to the streets. She became a drug addict and prostitute.

Growing up in the '90s, we had to go outside and stay outside until we were called in for dinner or when the street lights came on. What's funny is I didn't even know that we were poor. A white lady would come to our apartment, about every three months or so, to do an inspection. We would have to pretend that my aunt's daughter didn't live there. In reality, my brother and I shared a room, but when the white lady would come, I would have to lie and say my room was my cousin's room. We would clean up and make the house smell good—the scent of the original brand of Pine-Sol®.

Fortunately, we stayed in the front of the projects so we didn't get exposed to as much crime as the people in the back of the projects. Don't get me wrong, we still had our chairs out on the porch when there was a police chase, which was at least every two weeks. It was the highlight of the night, especially when the news showed up and we heard the sound of a helicopter searching from the sky for a wanted person. It felt like most of the kids lived in the back of the projects.

The Day Before My Aunt Gave Me Away

We were outside, this dark-skinned, skinny boy asked me and my brother if we wanted to play and we said "yes" with excitement. I had never met this boy before, nor did I ever see him around, but we played the rest of the day together.

As kids, you lose a lot of calories when playing, so we went to the boy's house to get a snack. His mother was home. My first impression of her was that she was kind of fat, like a teddy bear. She had a dimple. She was warm and had the biggest Kool-Aid smile that I had ever seen. She had long fingernails and smoked a cigarette while squinting her eyes and titling her head back so the smoke would not get in her pupils. Her voice was very raspy; she had one gold tooth in the front of her mouth.

"What is your name?" She asked.

"Toni Baker."

"What is your mother's name?" She questioned.

I told her, "Denise Baker."

Immediately she responded, "I know who your mother is and your people, and who your daddy is."

My eyes got big because I was confused like *how did this stranger know who my mother was, but most importantly, my father—how did she know?* I had been asking about my father's identity for years. I immediately lost my appetite, and all I wanted to do was run and go talk to my auntie. I told my brother David we had to go and we were out. I never had a chance to tell David what news I had discovered. I was in shock. I was nervous and kind of excited all at the same time. There were a lot of mixed feelings. I had been fantasizing for so long about what my dad looked like, or if I looked like him, or if he was some rich guy, or if I had other brothers and sisters. I had a long list of things that I would ask him if I ever had the chance to meet him. I knew why my mother wasn't present in my life, but I never knew why he wasn't there.

My Grandmother's House

The molesting continued for about three years. Nobody made sure I was properly cared for. I would go to school stinky and raggedy. Kids made fun of me. I already had a hard time because I had a boy's name and a mustache. They said I was a boy! Kids can be so cruel.

Around this time, I was in the third grade for the second time. I never remember anyone reading to me or asking me if I had homework. I could not read nor could I write, and my speech was at the level of a second grader. I had no idea I was doing so poorly. I would copy my friends' work at school and I got away with it, so who cared?

While in elementary school, I used to manage the after-school "snack" store. It was a program that the school put in place to give students opportunities and keep us out of trouble. I would steal money, candy, and chips and I thought I was getting away with that as well. However, my teacher (Mrs. Nosy Sunshine) was always in my business. She would do anything to keep me after school on most days. She always had a question for me. She always looked at me. Little did I know, she was really my angel.

The last time Hazel Eyes ever molested me was the worst of all. I remember begging him to just let me rest. That night, it stormed non-stop. I cried out to the Lord, even though at this time I didn't know that God really existed. I just needed something bigger, stronger, and more powerful to interrupt this moment. I wished so hard that he would not touch me, but he wanted what he wanted.

After several hours of hell, I was relieved when his sister came home, and that scared him away. Thank God! The horrible thing about the situation was that my grandmother's room was across from mine and she never heard anything.

When the interference from his sister came, he snuck out of my room and I went straight to the bathroom. There was blood everywhere, and it smelled like something died inside of me. My stomach ached so badly, and my head hurt as if someone knocked me out with a metal pole. I thought that maybe he shoved the gun too far inside me this time, and maybe that was why the blood would not stop. I kept wiping myself, but the blood just would not stop flowing from in between my legs. My underwear was full of blood, so I stuffed tissue in between my vagina and underwear. I wanted to take a shower, but it was the middle of the night, and I did not want to get into trouble. On my way out of the bathroom, I saw my female cousin. I rushed to my room and immediately changed my underwear and put the bloody pair under my mattress and tried to go to bed. That night, I slept in a ball as I always did once he was finished, but this time was different. I just could not shake the feeling.

The next day, I went to school and I was quiet as a mouse, more quiet than usual.

Here comes Little Mrs. Nosy Sunshine, my teacher. "Are you okay Toni?"

This time I could not hold back my tears, and I couldn't walk away from her or pretend she wasn't talking to me. I smelled bad and was in a lot of pain. I had to say something. I didn't know if I was pregnant or if I was going to die. I had never felt like this before and I was so scared. I told her everything! That's how I ascended through the pain and the struggle of being that little girl.

After telling my story over and over to the police, the doctor, and social services, I was exhausted and felt like no one believed me. They made me tell the story over and over again. All I wanted to do was scream and be alone. After several hours of what felt like being on trial, they finally told me that I was never going to see those people again. I was placed in the back of a police car and taken to the kids' shelter for months, then placed in the foster care system, and shortly thereafter, became a ward of the state.

Who would have known that this little girl who wished she was dead every day would be alive today; reading, writing, acting, hosting on big platforms, thriving as a radio host, and running her own television show called *Ascending with Toni Rochelle*? I am a mother of two talented, beautiful kids. I never gave up. The foster care system was my outlet to thrive.

Today, I live in the California Bay Area where my mission is to help as many people as I can to ascend through their struggles and help them to continue to rise, thrive, and prosper. My main focus is on foster care youth; particularly the ones who age out of the system to move on past their own pain and hurt, while helping them to build community and overcome all obstacles.

My brother and I finally saw each other again when I was a teenager. It had been years. He was so mad at me, because he felt like I abandoned him. When my auntie gave me away, I never had a chance to say good-bye. I couldn't call him. He had so many questions to ask me. Thank God he spread the questions out over the years. To this day, there are still things about my life that I am exposing to my brother. It has not been easy to build our relationship, but we both deal with the way our lives were set up.

Mr. Hazel eyes went to prison for what he did to me. I was smart to let the police know where all my underwear were hiding. I never had to see him again. I heard that he died in prison. I also never saw a single member from that family ever again.

My mother and I eventually reunited, and today, we celebrate her for being eleven years clean and serene, and counting.

I graduated high school and aged out of the foster care system. Then I was a part of the independent living program. I worked at Walmart while working as a stripper. I went to college and then moved to California when I turned twenty-one. While in California, I worked in corporate America for sixteen years, got married and divorced, and was fired during the pandemic when I became a single mother. During that time, I experienced homelessness, but I still ascended. What they broke in me, I rebuilt stronger. What they took, I reclaimed tenfold.

Reflections on Resilience

Life has a way of throwing us into situations we never asked for and forcing us to grow in ways we never thought possible. When the people who are supposed to protect and love us fail to do so, it can feel like the world is nothing but a cruel and lonely place. But even in those moments of darkness, there is something inside of us—small, quiet, but unyielding—that refuses to be extinguished. That is your light. It doesn't matter how small it feels or how dim it seems. That light is proof that you are still here, still standing, still capable of something more.

What you endured as a child was not your fault, and it was never a reflection of your worth. The pain, the betrayal, and the abandonment weren't meant to destroy you. Instead, those difficult experiences became the harsh teachers that forged your strength and compassion. You survived not because you had everything you needed, but because you found something within yourself that could not be broken, no matter how hard life tried. That part of you is your truth.

As you reflect on your story, remember this: survival is not the end of the journey—it is the foundation. From here, you get to decide how your life unfolds. You've taken your pain and turned it into purpose. You've proven that it is possible to rise from the ashes and create something beautiful. Now, what will you do with that light of yours? How will you use it to illuminate the paths of others? Because someone out there right now needs to see it's possible to ascend—just like you did.

TONI ROCHELLE was born and raised in Oklahoma City, Oklahoma. She is the oldest and the only girl of her mother's five children. Toni started writing when she became a ward of the state. She grew up in the foster care system and aged out of the system at eighteen. In 2005, she relocated to The Bay Area and immediately started modeling, appearing in fashion shows, magazines, and several (music) videos. Soon after, she started landing roles in independent films and stage plays. Her biggest accomplishments are acting in a Honda Commercial and the opportunity to perform at the Edinburgh Theater Festival in Scotland. Toni has established herself as a talk show host for the entertainment show "Off Tha Hook TV" on the OUR TV Network, where she shined while interviewing celebrities on the red carpet at The ASCAP awards, BET Awards pre-rooms, and different events in Los Angeles. She has interviewed entertainers such as Bobby Brown, Blair Underwood, and Smokey Robinson just to name a few. Toni has hosted many events, open mic nights, parties, and luncheons in The Bay Area. Her dreams and movements are inspired by God and her daughter Talia and son Tatum. She is further inspired by family, community, and friends. Toni's motto is to "keep *ascending* no matter what life throws at you." *Ascending with Toni Rochelle* inspires and empowers people to press through life's struggles and continue to rise, thrive, and prosper.

Toni has experience living through trauma, depression, and surviving many trials and tribulations and has the courage to share with the world through her own experiences.

CHAPTER 3

Noir Butterfly: Freedom in the Flight

by Tracye Burr

Blessed are you who hunger now, for you will be satisfied.
Blessed are you who weep now, for you will laugh.
—Luke 6:21 (NIV)

My marriage began unraveling twenty-five years ago, I just didn't see it. In August 2022, I ended my marriage in the Wegman's Cafe. After many months of arguing, my husband's hurled insults, my tears and screams, his infidelity, broken trust, sickness, and ill parents, I accepted that my husband wanted a divorce. It came down to us sitting in the cafe with our individual lists of "demands." We had been unable to resolve our differences through the attorney and this was a last resort.

Honestly, we did not reach much agreement. I caved on every issue as I typically had done. I was not always the best advocate for myself and despite the years of his infidelity, the narcissist behavior, and the "blame" game where all the troubles in the marriage were my fault, I walked away from that meeting at peace. I know many would wonder with all that was going on how could I be at peace. I can honestly say that it was because I heard the words "daughter, let go" and a warm feeling came over me; more importantly, a sense of relief after staring out of the window for what seemed like an eternity, but in fact was only a matter of seconds. I took a deep sigh, looked at my now ex and said "fine." I was utterly exhausted and tired of holding on to something and someone who did not want me. It was that voice that gave me strength to push back from the table and examine my worth.

Seven months earlier, I listened as my husband methodically explained why he wanted to divorce me; silently wishing that he would stop talking. What part of "my mother is dying" did he not hear? As I looked at his face, I only saw his mouth moving and did not react to the continual flow of sarcasm and cruelty that was being delivered. He wanted a girlfriend, someone to love him for him? What is he talking about? He was done with me?

As the tears slowly streamed down my face, partly from the anger, partly from the trauma of dealing with my sick mother for fifteen days, I could barely deliver a response or other emotions. I was in shock.

My mind kept going back to my life as a child. I longed to run away from anything controversial or upsetting. I was really good at pretending life's cruelties did not affect me and became very skilled at masking the deep feelings of uncertainty, low self-esteem, and often self-loathing.

During that moment, I silently watched the man I married nearly three decades ago aggressively shouting that he should have left me a long time ago and he only stayed in the marriage to be considered a hero. He's considered the favorite boy, the successful one—college graduate, former star athlete. He didn't want to be looked at as a failure, especially as it pertained to marriage. He cared more about his public façade than his private reality. During our conversation, he barely mentioned his numerous acts of infidelity, name calling, or the plain lack of interest in me or my needs; he seemed to love seeing me crumble. I felt like I was a sixteen-year-old girl again being belittled by my mother. This was an all-too-familiar feeling.

Emotionally, my deepest thoughts were pulling me to a place where I simply wanted to be invisible and blameless—I tried my hardest to be Perfect Patty, so that no one had anything negative to say about me. For so long, perfectionism had been my coping mechanism. If I over-achieved, *in my mind,* this would stop people from belittling me. This was a lie. I was scared. I was scared of disappointing my parents, my husband, my children, and my friends, but most of all, I was scared that I was not worthy of happiness or love. All these emotions flooded back to me at once during the conversation with my husband. Suddenly, I was alone, rejected, and my worst fears were my reality.

Beautifully Broken

Prior to my husband's uncontrollable emotional outburst, I had spent time with my mother in Arizona, helping to get her affairs in order. In a stunning turn of events, she had unceremoniously divorced my father of over fifty years to search for happiness in her small rural hometown in southern Arkansas—population 500. It made no sense to me, but my mother insisted and I tried my best to support her decision.

My relationship with my mom was complicated. While deep down, I knew my mother loved me, her idea of love came with an emotional toll on my self-esteem. Only now at the age of fifty-nine can I look at myself in the mirror and celebrate who I am and how far I have come.

Prior to leaving Arizona permanently, she insisted on staying at my dad's house. My mother was eighty-three, stubborn, and most of the time irrational in her decisions. It was nearly impossible to talk to her because my mother preferred to talk over you, curse you out, and bully you to the point of exhaustion.

Growing up, my mother's parenting style consisted of love with conditions. I either complied with her demands, or would be bullied and subjected to the silent treatment. I was frequently referred to as ugly, fat, selfish, or characterized as being unworthy of love. Of course mother was always apologetic after her outbursts, but that didn't remove the sting or the seeds of unworthiness that grew within me. On many occasions, Mom refused my phone calls, ignored my birthdays, and after I had my own children, she would ignore them as punishment for things she felt I had done.

I knew when I saw my mother this time that something was wrong—more than the usual irrational behavior. She was physically unstable, she was dragging her foot, and most of her conversations made no sense. I left Arizona not understanding what was going on but thought everything would be okay.

Unfortunately, after I had departed on my flight headed back to the East Coast, my mother fell backwards down the stairs, hit her head on the tile floor and was bleeding from her head. My father called the paramedics and they rushed her to the Emergency Room where after an MRI, the ER physician discovered a mass in her brain. My mother had a malignant brain tumor.

Hiding in Plain Sight

As a child, I always worked really hard to make sure I didn't give my parents any problems; especially my mother because her tongue was extremely bitter. I saw my mother lying on the couch smoking cigarettes for at least ten years of my life. She had no relationship with her own mother. While it seemed like she wanted to love me, the only way she knew how was to criticize me. To make the pain of not feeling love go away, I learned to adapt, accommodate, and disappear.

In spite of the pain, I always looked for a way to gain my mother's approval. I strived to be perfect—straight A's in school, went to the best university, got my master's degree, achieved the Dean's list, pledged Delta Sigma Theta Sorority, Incorporated, and became a member of The Links Incorporated and Jack and Jill of America. From the outside, it appeared I had it all. But on the inside there was fear, depression, and isolation.

I was silently killing myself to find love from my mom. That really backfired because when you're dealing with someone who hasn't dealt with their own pain, there's nothing you can do to make yourself appear better. They're always going to find something little to criticize you about; they're always picking at that thread, and unraveling and unraveling and unraveling, to the point that you begin to believe that you are not worthy. I spent many months in tearful therapy asking what was wrong with me. I thought I was doing everything right. Why doesn't she love me? I convinced myself to just keep trying harder. Unfortunately, I recognized that same behavior in my marriage.

Once I met my husband, I thought I found love and I started the habits of making sure he loved me. So what did I do? I learned to cook better, over-parented my three kids, picked them up from school, and helped with homework. I was the room mother and PTA President. I took care of the kids and washed the clothes. I tried to do whatever I could to make sure he loved me. I was accommodating when he worked late, helped in his business, ignored the infidelity, and concentrated more on being perfect for him and our kids. I was exhausted.

I stuffed myself into any role that I thought would make him love me. But I was never enough. He wanted more sex—no love-making, no connection, no intimacy. It became mechanical. He didn't want to talk to me. He couldn't talk unless we had sex first. He didn't want to hold my hand. He ignored phone calls and text messages. I began to feel like a sex object.

It was only after discovering the infidelity did I begin to truly unmask who he was. It wasn't just a solo cheating incident, but three—the childhood sweetheart, the college girlfriend, and the last and final straw, a woman with whom he conducted business. Every time I "caught" him curating those relationships, he took great effort in reassuring me I was wrong, apologizing and convincing me that I misunderstood the relationships.

If you ask him today if any of this is true, he would deny it and say I was wrong. But after a great deal of therapy, I realized he is a narcissist. Interestingly, I didn't know that narcissistic behavior included manipulation and they are very skilled at making themselves out to be the victim, similar to my mom. Again I had no idea who he really was. I was looking for love and thought he was the right one. But now, knowing who he is, and seeing the cruelty, and how he reacts to me—that's not love.

Love is a Verb or Adjective—You Decide

Listening to my husband's rant caused me to think about LOVE. *What is love?* Is love a verb? Is it a noun? Is it an attitude? Is it a belief, or is it nonexistent? Over the past two years I've asked myself that question hundreds of times, and I concluded that love is a verb; it's an action—beyond just saying and verbalizing—it's doing. And love not only includes how I feel about another person, but how I feel about myself.

A big part of my journey has been learning to love me for me. It took a lot of therapy, but I finally began to realize that I am lovable and I'm not perfect, which is fine. Self-love includes learning that not everyone in your life is worth fighting for and that's OK. Soon after my husband's announcement, and on the advice of my therapist, I started journaling. I wrote him a letter that he will never read; expressing all the love, disappointments, and anger with our relationship. This one act opened a door of emotions for me. That letter is ridiculously long, filled with spelling errors and a whole lot of anger, but it helped me crack the door to my emotional healing and releasing all of the negative energy I was holding.

Measuring My Worth by Someone's Else's Standards

Back to the here and now, as I listened to my husband's ranting, I couldn't help but think about how I cared for him when he started having unexplainable seizures five years prior. I took care of him, took him to doctor appointments, wiped him down when he soiled himself, helped him in his business all while working full-time, helping my three children with their homework, being a mom, and standing in while my husband was in crisis. I was exhausted, mentally and physically. I too needed someone to support me. On top of his seizures and carrying the full weight of our household *alone*, I had just learned my mother was terminally ill. When I received that news, my husband walked out of the door to attend a "festival" in his hometown—five hours away.

As things began to unravel more, the man I married double-downed on his efforts to break me mentally and emotionally and made it known that he had no intentions of stopping his extra-marital affairs. Instead he lied and pretended that these relationships were just friends and that they were helping him understand how to relate to ME which I called BULL.

Slowly, I began to realize that I was striving so hard to live up to someone else's expectations of me and that I was fighting for someone that was not fighting for me. I spent many days trying to figure out what was wrong with me, and it made me think of my childhood and dealing with my mother and trying to be perfect. I was trying to live up to the expectations that someone else had placed on me. All throughout this journey of trying to figure out me, I forgot how to love me. How did I get here?

So what's my lesson to share? Learn to love yourself. I am a great friend, a great listener, a great mom, and have people who love me in my life. Don't get me wrong, I do have my faults but I married someone who didn't see me. If it wasn't about me having sex with him, he was not interested in me. Something as simple as *let's go for a walk* was shut down. I remember talking about our twenty-fifth wedding anniversary and wanting to plan a quick trip and the response I got was, "Why would I want to do anything with you?" That single sentence shattered me in a way that I couldn't explain.

God put me here for a purpose, and I was not meant to accept less than I deserved—His best. More importantly, like a butterfly emerging from the darkness, I realized I had to shed the expectations to grow my wings. I remind myself of a sermon by T. D. Jakes about expectations, "Once a person teaches me who they are, they have taught me what to expect, that's why I can never be disappointed or expect more than the person is advertising..." that is a tough lesson. Changing my expectations of my husband and my mother freed me from frustration, disappointments, and hurt. I cannot expect what they cannot give. I wasn't just leaving a marriage, I was reclaiming myself piece-by-piece from the broken shards of my past.

Holding On and Letting Go at the Same Time Doesn't Work

I honestly was so broken between my husband and my mother I cried for three weeks. During my weeping days, I prayed and wept. And it was during that period I finally let go of all those expectations. I would never get the answers to my questions about why she was so mean to me, why had my husband cheated, or why neither of them loved me. I would never get those answers. The closure I needed wasn't in their hands, it was in mine.

I talked with my therapist and she only asked me one profound question, "Why did I forget about me?" She reminded me that there was so much beauty within me and that I was brilliant. I had a brain and I was worthy of love. Instead of confronting those things that haunted and bothered me, why had I spent the better part of my life as a grown woman in the fetal position, scared, unable to move, and afraid that I would disappoint others. I will never forget when she said, "You are a soft and gentle spirit." I am like a butterfly, beautiful, yet unable to embrace her beauty because she simply cannot see her wings. I realized that letting go was healing for me one day at a time.

I Didn't Know My Own Strength

There are many days that I can't shake the sorrow that I feel for the loss of my marriage and this journey has given me a chance to learn more about myself. I have taken a lot of time journaling and reflecting to figure out who I am, and embracing all the best parts of me so as not to let anyone else break me. I consciously surround myself with people who are positive, who are willing and want to see me succeed, and not those that are willing to knock me down. I have lost some friends, but I've had some really amazing friends who stayed in my life and who have pushed me beyond my comfort zone. They've accepted the best parts of me while acknowledging that there are things that I need to work on.

I'm an over-thinker. I ask a lot of questions, and I hold a lot of things in, but I'm learning to talk about my feelings, learning to love all of the best parts of me, and even learning not to start my day without giving thanks to the Creator for waking me up and giving me another chance to live in my purpose. I also learned to stop collecting Red Flags for the empty vase in the window. Red flags are those things that pop up and your inner voice is telling you *RUN GIRL RUN*! Red flags were popping up all over the place in my marriage and because of my own emotional insecurities, I just ignored them.

I think about love and I believe that the right person will be waiting for me when God says it's time. In this season of waiting, I am focused on healing emotionally, building my confidence, and learning to love me, flaws and all.

Reflections on Resilience

Life often places us in situations that demand we choose between holding on and letting go. Sometimes, the hardest lesson to learn is that not everyone in our lives is meant to stay. Loving yourself is not selfish—it is necessary. It is the foundation that allows you to let go of people and situations that no longer serve your growth. Love is not just an action you give others; it's also a gift you give yourself. Ask yourself: Am I loving myself as deeply as I deserve?

When you've spent your life trying to live up to the expectations of others, you can lose sight of who you are. The need to be perfect, to be loved, or to be enough can overshadow your true worth. But your worth is not defined by what others think or how they treat you. Your worth is inherent, unshakable, and untouchable. It is in the way you rise after every fall, in the courage you show by stepping into the unknown, and in the quiet strength you find to heal.

As you move forward, remember this: healing is not a destination—it's a journey. Each day brings a chance to learn more about yourself, to celebrate who you are, and to release what no longer aligns with your spirit. Surround yourself with people who uplift you, honor your light, and remind you of your value.

This book was released after the death of my mom, Emery Evans, which brought a deeper sense of grief than I can explain. As my mother passed from this life, I did my best to clear her conscious. I whispered, "I love you despite my pain and I release you with no regrets. Rest well."

TRACYE BURR is a novice writer with a passion for reading and sharing stories that create a voice for women who are experiencing life in some-times unimaginable circumstances. Her mantra is to leave any situation or interaction better than she found it regardless of how large or small the action may be.

Professionally, Tracye is a seasoned marketing professional with a passion for pioneering brand strategies that resonate. With the ability to navigate the ever-evolving landscape, she seeks to promote outcomes that speak to the customer by showcasing untapped needs, multicultur-al perspectives, and creativity that captures the essence of needs of the diverse consumer groups she represents. Tracye thrives on delivering exemplary marketing outcomes with measurable success driven from data and market insights.

Tracye resides in Mesa, Arizona. She is a recent divorcee and the mother of three phenomenal children (Joseph III, Olivia, and Lauryn) and grandmother of one super cute grandson whom she adores.

Tracye holds a BS in Managerial Economics from U.C. Davis and an MBA/MSM in Marketing from the University of Maryland. Tracye is an active Diamond Life Member of Delta Sigma Theta Sorority, Incorporated, The Links Incorporated, and a member of Kingdom Fellowship AME Church.

In her free time, Tracye is an avid reader, a foodie who lives to create in the kitchen, and when time permits likes to travel internationally but most importantly treasures spending quality time with her family and circle of sister friends. Tracye's favorite quote by Maya Angelou is *"People will forget what you said, people will forget what you did, but people will never forget how you made them feel."*

CHAPTER 4

Resilience in the Valley: Facing Grief from Both Life and Death

by Denise Rollins, PhD

As I sat at my eighty-six-year-old father's bedside, the room was calm. He was sleeping, yet there was a war raging inside me. I had decided that year to focus on building my faith, so despite the slim chances my father's doctor gave him, and regardless of the obvious weakened state of his body, I believed Dad when he said that he was going to fight. I also believed that if my faith was strong enough, we'd both make it to the other side of this test, and we'd testify about how good God is. "Come on, Denise, you cannot waiver. You must believe." I kept coaching myself with those words. I spoke life. I spoke prosperity. I spoke health over my earthly father! And I kept calling on Jesus and refusing to believe that I was being thrust in the valley of the shadow of death, again.

My first season in that valley happened between ages eight and twenty-one with the illness-induced deaths of my three grandparents, uncle, and aunt. Back then, no one helped us kids understand death and grief. So, I was left with an unspoken sadness that felt like my constant, secret companion. That sadness took center stage again, right before my thirtieth birthday, and had a starring role for the next fifteen years.

I remember the day death and grief reappeared as if it were yesterday. After all, it was the day I died.

On that day, June 2, 1995, my beautiful mother was forty-nine years young, and I was twenty-nine. That Friday night, I was her date when she was honored at a company dinner. On the drive home, Mom was reflective as she told me how fleeting life could be. She talked about someone who died instantly when she was hit by a car that crossed the center line and even told me where I'd find her will if anything ever happened to her. At twenty-nine, I wasn't ready for that conversation, so I quickly changed the topic. I dropped Mom off at her car, and she went to pick up my sister then headed home.

A short time later, I answered my phone and heard my Aunt Flora screaming for me to come to the hospital. Upon arrival, I was led to a side room where my aunt and sister sobbed as they told me a drunk driver had crossed the center line and taken Mom's life. I collapsed, unable to process that reality. My mother was my best friend, confidante, and role model. I was not ready to navigate life without her.

That day, Mom wasn't the only one who died; the person I was prior to her passing also died in many ways. With her death, I lost my way, unsure of who I was without her. Today, I realize it was in the shadow of death and in the depth of my grief that I began my quest to find my purpose. Pain can sometimes do that. Filled with sadness, rage, pity, confusion, and other overwhelming and raw emotions, I found a therapist who helped me through that dark period. Yet I still felt so powerless. The daily headaches I felt after Mom's death were an outward sign of inward wounds that I felt would never heal.

My thirtieth birthday is a blur because it happened right after my mom was killed. Ten years later, what made my fortieth birthday memorable was the fact that two months earlier I had given birth to my fourth son, Isaiah. I had no plans to have another child, but along came this blessing who changed my life. With Isaiah's older brothers, I quickly returned to work after giving birth, focused on climbing the corporate ladder. But the combination of being older, self-employed, and having such an unexpected gift, made me slow down and cherish each moment with my newborn. I'm grateful now that I took that time because I never could have predicted what would happen next.

On a beautiful and unseasonably warm September morning, I woke up to the smell of bacon cooking. Downstairs, my husband, Ralph, was making breakfast, and our four sons were seated around the kitchen table. All of them looked adorable but it was my youngest, Isaiah, at five months, who stole the show. The other boys (ages seven, ten, and thirteen at the time) were hurriedly eating before leaving school. Isaiah was his usual smiling, happy self. I had to rush off to a meeting at my office, so my husband said that since he was working from home, he'd take our seven-year-old, Malcolm, to school and Isaiah to daycare. Because the breakfast put us behind schedule, instead of Ralph dropping Isaiah off first, he switched his routine and took our third son to school first.

When he got back to our neighborhood, he saw a tow truck entering the community and knew it was there to pick up the van we were donating to charity. Later that afternoon, after handling the donation and working from home, Ralph left the house to pick Isaiah up from daycare. To his horror, he realized that Isaiah was still in the car. He had never dropped off Isaiah at school and he had been in the car for several hours.

Ralph was frantic when he called me to rush home. As soon as I walked through the door, paramedics hit me with the news that our baby didn't make it. This was September 2005. While the rest of the world was witnessing Hurricane Katrina, my family was thrust into its own deadly storm. As I dealt with my grief this time, it was complicated by helping the kids understand an unconscionable loss and trying to comfort a husband who was in unimaginable pain. That pain was magnified as he was prosecuted for a mistake any of us could have made, and for which he was already punishing himself far more than any criminal sentence could achieve.

As a family that was extremely private, our loss thrust us into a harsh spotlight that taught us a lot about unfairly judging others and even more about humility. "Take all the kids away from those terrible parents," read one editorial. A close friend said she couldn't stand to be around my husband because of what had happened. Didn't she know that he had been a better and more attentive parent than me and that he would never do anything like this on purpose? We pulled together as a family, each of us completed therapy, and we slowly healed.

Yet grief has a way of creating a "hole" in our hearts that, when unaddressed, will rob us of life. As I look back now, I realize how much each of us had either dismissed the deadliness of our "holes", or tried to fill them with things that were more detrimental. With Isaiah's passing came so much more pain, a sense of having even less power, and an inability to find any purpose in the tragic death of a child.

Following Isaiah's death, I mourned deeply and silently. By January 2007, I had finally begun to get myself together when, on a beautiful Saturday morning, I was stopped in my tracks by a phone call notifying me and my sister that our Aunt Flora, who was my mother's sister and a surrogate mom to me since my mother's death, had been killed as a result of her car being hit by someone who was drag racing on a public road.

In addition to sorrow, I think my predominant emotion at the time was anger. After all, how much could one family take? When I reflect on that period, I'm struck by the depth of my grief yet how few people knew how hard Aunt Flora's death had hit me. In the world's eyes, she was "just" my aunt. But I wasn't grieving her title, I was grieving her role in my life and the close relationship we had.

I began to feel heightened grief over my mom and Isaiah all over again. Yet I kept it to myself. Back then, there were times I felt invisible in my grief. Instead of sharing my pain with others, I wore a mask and compressed my emotions, which was becoming a pattern for me. Sadly, pushing down my pain actually made it stronger and took away my power.

Then, in the shadow of that valley, my heart was shattered once again. On June 9, 2009, at the tender age of forty-nine, my husband, Ralph, father of our four sons, died suddenly from the complications of sickle cell disease. Unofficially, I believe he died from a broken heart. His grief was too much for him to bear and, as a result, our sons (then ages eleven, fourteen, and seventeen) and I lost our rock.

Therapy helped, but I also realized that other life changes were needed. I'd been so focused on getting through all these deaths that I was barely living. To say that I was broken after Ralph's passing is an understatement. I was also battling with the cumulative effect of so many deaths of people who'd played pivotal roles in shaping my outlook, boosting my confidence, and affirming my choices. That was compounded by a lifetime of struggles of feeling inadequate, unloved, and unliked. Due to the loss of crucial people, as well as the absence of self-esteem and joy, my spirit was broken, and my heart was wounded as I laid in the valley of the shadow of death, grief, and despair.

I believe that bad things sometimes happen to good people and there's not always a reason attached, which is painful. Yet our power comes in choosing to use those bad things (in my case, so many deaths) to do something good in the world. This choice allows us to take back our power and even find our purpose.

That's what happened to me at age forty-four, following Ralph's death. I'd reached a crossroad and asked myself a profound question: If I knew that I had only five more years to live because I would die at forty-nine as both my husband and mother had, would I continue the path I was on? The answer was a quick and resounding no.

I know now that my answer was fueled by grief from death, but also by grief from life. This included disappointments with my career, the way I was treated, and the impact I wanted to make. So, despite a lucrative six-figure paycheck and five-figure bonus, perks like a company car and exotic trips, and the prestige of being in a consulting role with an industry leader, I decided that my peace was priceless, my purpose was elsewhere, and it was time to begin planning to pursue another path. Nine months later, I shocked everyone by resigning to pursue my new life.

Almost a year later, I had the most incredible weekend ever, much of which I hadn't imagined one year before. First, on Friday, May 18, I married Gary Rollins on the six-month anniversary of our first date. We'd both buried a spouse (his wife died five months after my husband) and were passionate about helping people deal with loss (as a funeral director, Gary understood and believed in my dream of opening a grief center). On Saturday, May 19, I graduated with a Master of Science in Thanatology, the psychological study of grief and death. And on Sunday, May 20, we attended a phenomenal church that we later joined, then drove to Philadelphia so that on Monday, May 21 I'd begin working on a PhD in Marriage and Family Therapy. Life was pretty good!

The ten-year gap between that dream weekend in 2012 and 2022, when I sat by my father's bedside, felt like a blink of an eye. Dad fought hard. I prayed hard. So did everyone else. And yet, on August 18, 2022, as we sat beside his bed and prayed for life, Dad took his last earthly breath. I cried enough tears to drown myself in that valley of death. I realize now that I would have never been ready to say goodbye to the man whose love for me was boundless. Dad always greeted me with a huge smile saying, "Hello, my daughter," and then parted with a hug and, "I love you, my daughter." I felt robbed!

When my son got seriously ill within days of Dad's passing, I can tell you that there was a moment when I felt like I'd lost my faith. Watching Dad's last breath and witnessing Malcolm's health struggles weighed heavily on my heart. My father and my son formed the book-ends of my life.

Yet in reflecting on the life of my father, the stories people told about him at his funeral, and the emotions that his passing evoked for so many, I was struck by how wholeheartedly he lived his eighty-six years and ten months on this earth. He tried new things, took risks that allowed him to make a difference, told people how he felt about them (both good and bad), and lived with a sense of gratitude. One of his many sayings was, "every day's a new day!" Dad's death showed me that as much as I encouraged others to embrace life wholeheartedly, I didn't necessarily practice what I preached. The proof was in my son's hospital stay.

Malcolm, my third son, is undoubtedly the child with whom I have the tightest emotional bond due in part to the ways we drew closer after the deaths of his brother and father. In the early days of those losses, when Malcolm was a pre-teen, his pain became my pain as he expressed and worked through his grief. Yet during his late teens and early twenties, my pain became his pain as my overprotectiveness and fear of losing another child began to smother him.

During his hospitalization in 2018, I had an epiphany that his illness was caused in part by my fears and pain. Malcolm inherited my love of learning, my desire to make a difference, and other good things. But I'd also given him my brokenness. In hindsight, I realize that this knowledge wasn't enough for me to change both my feelings and behaviors as much as I needed to. Now, I can clearly see that while my father had epitomized my definition of L.I.F.E. (Living Intentionally, Fearlessly, and Expectantly), I instead was projecting the opposite on my child. I was showing him D.E.A.T.H. (Destructive Emotions, Actions, Thoughts, and Habits) and it was draining both his soul and mine.

With Dad's passing, I grieved death. Yet with Malcolm's illness, I grieved life. Merriam-Webster's dictionary defines grief as "deep and poignant distress caused by or as if by bereavement." Bereavement is described as "the state or fact of being bereaved or deprived of something or someone." In reacting to both situations, I had deep and poignant distress due to being deprived of someone (my father) and something (Malcolm's good health). Either way, I knew that grief was slowly draining me of life, just as it had when I walked away from my corporate job.

Dad gave me life. But why couldn't I fully live it? Why couldn't I give that same wholehearted life to my son, Malcolm, his siblings, and the world? People often speak of standing in the valley of the shadow of death. I was stuck in that valley and felt I'd never make my way out. I began to see myself as the person that death happens to, which is a sad perspective.

When I finally began to separate my heart and mind from that fateful place, I realized that it was just as painful to be stuck in the valley of the shadow of life. The same painful grief that comes with death and the loss of people we love can also be felt when we experience other life changes and/or disappointments. From the loss of relationships or jobs to the lack of self-esteem and missed opportunities, or even good things like a child going away to school or a new marriage, many of us are unconsciously grieving life's changes or conflicts. That type of grief can plague our minds and hurt our hearts.

In 2022, after the physical death of my beloved father and during the brief illness of my son, I stood at yet another crossroad. When I walked away from corporate America, it was mostly due to external factors that weren't healthy for my heart and mind. After Dad's death, I discovered that I also had to separate myself from internal thoughts and feelings that poisoned my mind and heart and kept me from living fully.

I again had the outer trappings of success but not enough inner joy. To truly choose life over death this time, I had to address my internal conflicts by doing serious work on my mind and my heart; massaging them with grace, mercy, and peace. I needed to see the good in myself, others, and God. While I know everything won't always work out as I desire, I am grounded in faith, rather than fear. I must constantly uplift myself while stopping the self-sabotage and projecting of my fears and failures on my sons and others. I must take my power back and choose life, a daily process that includes both baby steps and quantum leaps.

This new and wholehearted way to live would help me fulfill my purpose. Instead of looking around me at problems, which in 2022 included my dad's death and my son's health struggles, I looked upward to my Problem Solver. It was then that I realized how much my perspective needed to shift. Stuck in the Valley, I learned to look upward for strength, transforming my sorrow into purpose.

Rather than carrying burdens alone, believing that if I had prayed enough or lived more nobly my dad would still be here and my son wouldn't have gotten ill, I had to look up at God, give my burdens to Him, and see my life (including my struggles) from His perspective. And I can't just do that one time; I must do it repeatedly.

When I think on what is good, right, and noble, my mind and heart begin to align, and gratitude emerges. Now, don't misunderstand me; I'm not grateful that my father passed away. I still grieve his absence. I strongly believe that we may never get over certain losses (with me, I'll always miss my father), but we can get through grief with work and intentionality. I'm grateful that Dad's no longer in pain. I'm fulfilled, knowing he's asleep in Christ. And I'm overjoyed that I had fifty-seven exceptional years with Dad, learned so much from him, and have so many precious memories.

I now start each day giving God my heart and mind, knowing I can live intentionally, fearlessly, and expectantly with power and purpose, and in honor of the man whose life taught me to do just that. And from that posture, my sons get the lessons I learned from my earthly father, who gave me a glimpse of the love that's always been there from my Heavenly Father. It's been said that the height of our joy is only matched by the depth of our sorrow. Both my great joys and great sorrows helped me overcome both external and internal challenges. The losses I faced and the pain I experienced have shaped me and led me to my purpose.

Moving forward, I'll continue to nurture my spirit at times when I'm grieving either death or life because I'm human. After all, grief is the price of love. And while I might visit the valley, I won't get stuck there because I have the power, perspective, and process to live wholeheartedly! I am grateful for that resilience! Grief taught me that life, even in its harshest valley, is a gift worth embracing.

Reflections on Resilience

Grief is a profound and universal experience. It comes in many forms—not just the loss of loved ones but also the loss of dreams, health, relationships, or even identities we once cherished. Yet within the depths of grief lies a choice: to remain stuck in the valley or to find a path toward purpose. What we often fail to recognize is that grief and love are two sides of the same coin. The more we love, the more deeply we grieve. And while the pain may never fully fade, it can transform into something meaningful if we allow it.

When life thrusts us into the valleys of despair, it can feel like an endless shadow. But even in the darkest places, we can choose to look upward. Grief is not a linear process, nor is healing. Both require grace, patience, and intention. It's okay to sit with your sorrow, but don't unpack and live there. Start with small steps—whether it's speaking to someone you trust, journaling your feelings, or simply taking a moment to breathe deeply and remind yourself that you're still here.

Remember, grief is not just a testament to what we've lost—it's also a reminder of what we've had. Each tear shed honors the love and connection that shaped us. Each moment of resilience honors the life we are still living. As you move forward, give yourself permission to grieve fully and love fully, knowing that both are essential parts of the human experience. In your greatest sorrow, you may just find your greatest strength.

DR. DENISE ROLLINS is a coach to women. She is committed to helping herself, her clients, sisters, family, friends, and sorors to become whole-hearted in Living Intentionally, Fearlessly, and Expectantly (L.I.F.E). In the intersection of her personal experience, Dr. Denise has discovered how much we silently struggle in grieving the deaths of significant people in our lives, while also facing the grief associated with other life changes and events. She learned these lessons amidst the tragic and sudden deaths of her mom, baby, aunt, and husband; in leadership roles with a Fortune 100 company; co-ownership of two businesses; non-profit executive director roles with the Whole Heart Grief & Life Resource Center and the Black Health Equity Coalition, and even a stint as a L.I.F.E. coach on The Real Housewives of Potomac. She earned an MS in Thanatology, which is the study of grief and death, and a PhD in Marriage and Family Therapy.

Dr. Denise is known for her spiritual discernment (as one who humbly seeks to walk in her eternal purpose). Hence, part of Dr. Denise's calling includes connecting with the women who take care of everyone else so that they too may process their grief from both death and life by addressing their pain, reclaiming their power, and pursuing their purpose.

CHAPTER 5

Dreams Birthed in Disappointment

by Trina Wiggins, M.D.

It was January 12, 1980, and the energy was electric as Ujamaa dorm packed into Maples Pavilion to cheer on Stanford Women's Gymnastics. For many of my dormmates, it was their first time watching a meet, and I felt the weight of their expectations, along with those of my coaches and fans. We were facing the powerhouse USC team, ranked fifth in the nation, and the crowd was one of the largest ever to witness a gymnastics event at Stanford. I was up second on vault—my favorite event—and though my stomach fluttered with nerves, I kept repeating my mantra: *You got this. Stick it.* As I chalked up my hands and waited for the judges› signal, I knew this moment had the potential to be unforgettable.

I sprinted down the runway with adrenaline surging as I launched into my vault, striking it with an ensuing powerful push-off that propelled me into the air. Mid-air, I sensed it was one of my best—powerful and clean. Now, all I had to do was control the landing. As I descended, I aimed for a solid landing but was forced to take a slight forward step to maintain balance. Looking up, I saw Maples Pavilion erupting with cheers—my Ujamaa dormmates, family, and fans all on their feet, celebrating. Not only had I secured first place in the vault, but I also set a new Stanford Women's Gymnastics record. It was the perfect start to our season, with Hawaii as our next destination.

Once we arrived in Hawaii, my teammates and I wasted no time immersing ourselves in the local scene. We enjoyed some downtime before the meet, savoring the novelty of our surroundings. Eager to make the most of our time, we hit the gym for practice routines the next day. The energy was electric, and I felt on top of my game, successfully executing all my routines on the bars, balance beam, vault, and floor exercise. Needless to say, I was on a high leaving the gym that day.

The next morning, I went through my familiar mental workout and stretching routine—nothing out of the ordinary. As the meet kicked off, I started on the balance beam. Beginning with the beam was a personal choice. I loved it because I could tackle the most nerve-wracking event right from the get-go and get it out of the way. I was ready!

With the judge's nod, I began my routine by mounting the balance beam with a front tuck. I executed the mount and landed it without a wobble–yeah! At this point, I felt great; I had one trick down and three more to go. I danced to the end of the beam, preparing for my next move—a standing back tuck. I was confident because I had nailed this move countless times before, but this time, something felt different. As I thrust myself into the air, the takeoff felt good, but a subtle sensation of unease rippled through me as I landed. It was a split-second feeling, but that was enough to seal my fate. The next thing I knew, I was writhing in agony on the floor, clutching my right knee. I immediately knew this was not good. One miscalculated takeoff brought me crashing to the floor, rendering me immobile.

The tears came naturally—an obvious mix of frustration and physical pain. In that heart-wrenching moment, I still yearned to perform my routines and captivate the crowd with my skill, but the reality was inescapable. It was not meant to be.

The paramedics swiftly arrived and transported me to the nearest urgent care facility. Once there, X-rays were immediately taken. I remember thinking then that, thankfully, I had no bones broken. Little did I know that this initial assessment would pale in comparison to the more severe injury and lifelong complications I would suffer.

The training staff on site informed me that surgery would be necessary once I returned to Stanford. In the meantime, I was given pain medication and placed on a plane with my knee encased in a stabilization brace. The relief from the pain medication was short-lived. After it wore off, I had to endure a persistent throb during the grueling six-hour flight. The flight attendants were kind enough to allow me to sit in first class so I could stretch my legs out. Nonetheless, it felt like the longest flight of my life.

Soon after landing, I was rushed into surgery. I remember waking up with a full-length cast stretching from the upper thigh to the ankle—my new reality for the next twelve weeks. The practical challenges of not being able to use my leg became apparent almost immediately. Now I was worried about other things that had nothing to do with performing. How would I manage the simplest tasks, like going to the bathroom? How would I get to class since I couldn't ride my bike? How could I even get food? Well, let's just say I figured it out.

When the day finally arrived for the cast to be removed, I had to commit to a lengthy rehabilitation process. The goal was to regain functionality and strength in my injured leg. Eventually, the moment arrived when I needed to make a tough decision to either continue my gymnastics career or retire from the sport. Let me tell you, even after such a terrible accident, a part of me still wanted to stick with gymnastics. Up until that point, it had been my whole life. However, the reality was that it was too risky, and I needed to do what was best for my body. Once I let go of my dream of striving to reach higher goals within the sport of gymnastics, my new life path led me toward a career in medicine.

Even after my competitive gymnastics days were behind me, I remained dedicated to maintaining my fitness. While in medical school, I met a wonderful man who became my husband and shared my commitment to fitness. This man—a former football player for Vanderbilt University—had undergone the same knee injury as I did. Remarkably, we both decided to retire from our respective sports and be intentional about sustaining our fitness levels while channeling our passion into the world of medicine.

Our connection was deeper than our shared injury experiences. We recognized the value of maintaining an active lifestyle, even as medical school demanded our full attention. Our days were consumed by rigorous coursework and demanding schedules, yet we refused to allow our careers to compromise our commitment to health and wellness.

After completing medical school, my husband and I decided to start a family, and we were doubly blessed with the arrival of twin boys. The responsibilities and joys of parenthood transformed our lives, and I was happier than I had ever been. Life was so beautiful and peaceful.

Early one morning, while carrying each of our twins on my hips and walking toward the kitchen, my bad knee buckled beneath me, and before I knew it, I was on the floor. It all happened so fast that my mind was in a haze, trying to figure out what had happened. Despite the disorientation, my maternal instinct kicked in. My top priority was comforting my crying sons, pushing my own discomfort aside for the moment. Once they were settled, I scooted to the refrigerator to grab the breast milk for my boys. The next step was to get to my phone. I crawled to the phone and called my husband, Carl, to tell him what happened.

He wasted no time, rushing home with a pair of crutches so I could be mobile again. Still, the pressing question remained—what on earth had just happened, and how would I care for our twins with a busted knee? We were now in a dilemma as our family wasn't nearby to help us care for the boys.

I swiftly arranged an appointment with the orthopedic surgeon to determine the cause of this setback. Upon consultation, the doctor ordered an MRI, and the results revealed the disheartening news that I had once again torn my ACL.

The gravity of the situation wasn't lost on me. I knew the surgery and subsequent recovery from this procedure would be quite difficult now that I was a mom. It's one thing to endure surgery without the responsibilities of caring for kids, but having two active toddlers in the mix would be a true test.

With my upcoming surgery in mind, I formulated a plan. I decided to confine my twins to a designated area in our home before the procedure. I knew I couldn't afford the physical strain of chasing them all over the house. So, I invested in a Walmart fence, hoping it would help contain their boundless energy during my recovery. Unfortunately, this initial attempt didn't work out as planned since the twins escaped it more times than I could count.

Plan B! I enlisted the help of professionals to construct a wrought iron fence encircling our living room. Within this newly designated space, I went to great lengths to childproof the environment and ensure their safety. At the heart of this modified living room, I placed a jungle gym to help them burn up all their energy and give me a few moments of rest.

Next, I strategically placed my office and workout equipment outside the borders of the play area so I could easily keep an eye on them. This arrangement turned out to be more beneficial than I ever imagined, as I could maintain a semblance of productivity and self-care even during my recovery period. The unexpected silver lining was that my twins began to mimic my exercises, using the jungle gym as their own exercise station. This unfortunate injury transformed a challenging situation into a bonding opportunity as we exercised together. Over time, the healing process took its course. With patience and diligence, my knee mended, and I regained strength in my leg once again.

As the twins transitioned into the early years of elementary school, I stumbled upon a new sport that would change my life forever. Back in 2003, during my sister's hunt for a wedding venue in Las Vegas, a chance encounter changed everything for me. At the Rio Resort and Casino, a colossal sign bearing the words "Ms. Fitness USA" caught our attention. With some time to spare due to the wedding planner's delay, we decided to wander in and see what was going on. What we stumbled upon was nothing short of phenomenal. Ms. Fitness USA was a fitness competition where women engaged in routines reminiscent of gymnastics, delivered speeches in stunning evening gowns, and modeled bikini swimwear. It was the most fascinating thing I had seen since my days as a gymnast. In a spur-of-the-moment challenge from my sister, I was all in! Once I returned home, I started the preparation to compete in Ms. Fitness USA. Little did I know that this decision would continue to shape my journey even today, as I continue to work hard and captivate audiences with my performances, which I always dreamed of doing.

After several years in the competition circuit, I began training to learn new tricks to incorporate into my routine. I distinctly recall the day when all my training efforts culminated in success. I had finally perfected a challenging routine! With the practice session winding down, I was determined to push myself just a little bit further because I knew I could do more. I nailed my last trick of the day! However, just as I stepped off the mat, I heard that ominous pop—the very same sound I remembered from that fateful day in Hawaii. In a moment of frustration, all I could muster was an exasperated, "SHIT." The fear of déjà vu was overwhelming. All I could think was 'Not again.'

Just five months remained until the national championships—an event I was determined to participate in to showcase my new skills— and I knew something had gone wrong again. Nervously heading to the orthopedic doctor once again, I awaited confirmation of my fears. Indeed, his diagnosis confirmed what I already knew—another torn ACL. Though infuriated by the setback, I shifted my energy toward a swift recovery, determined to be back on track within just four months. I outlined a meticulous plan, setting goals to lead me to prime condition by showtime. This time, I was not going to give up.

My approach to healing was multifaceted and intensive. Rehabilitation took center stage, complemented by cryotherapy, contrast therapy, massage, cupping, and dry needling. I explored every avenue to ensure that this obstacle wouldn't extinguish the flames of my dreams as it had done in 1980. Approaching my late forties, I was quite aware of the natural decline in strength, endurance, and flexibility, so I had to keep going to maintain my level of fitness.

While in this holding pattern, waiting for my knee to heal, I turned to creative strategies to maintain my physical activity and overall endurance. One afternoon, while entering my garage, a glint of something caught my attention in the corner of my eye—one of the twins' skateboards. My mind began to race with possibilities, and I quickly retrieved the skateboard and brought it into the house. I envisioned an unconventional workout, which entailed propping my injured leg on the skateboard to take a ride as I rowed with my good leg. This new physical activity was a brilliant idea that I could not wait to implement! It was a game-changer in keeping my fitness level on par. As my knee healed, I was determined not to let my fitness progress stall.

In a remarkable twist, I converted my injury-induced limitations into an unexpected advantage. This phase of recovery provided an opportunity to perfect my handstands. With my legs temporarily out of commission, I dedicated myself to honing this skill. It was a training avenue that didn't require my legs and offered a unique chance to make the most of my circumstances. As the months progressed, my knee gradually regained its strength and function. Remarkably, within a span of four months, I found myself once again ready to compete and showcase my newly acquired skills. The competition season turned out to be a fruitful one. In the Ms. Fitness USA competition, I secured a spot in the top 10—a testament to my dedication and adaptability. This achievement propelled me forward, setting the stage for an even greater victory several years later—capturing the title of Fitness America Classic.

Reflections on Resilience

It is important to remember that while life's challenges—such as injuries or unforeseen setbacks—can alter our paths, they do not define our destinies. Instead, these obstacles can serve as catalysts for growth, leading us to discover new passions, forge deeper connections, achieve goals we hadn't envisioned, and inspire others to achieve their dreams. Setbacks are not endpoints but rather opportunities for reinvention.

DR. TRINA WIGGINS is a board-certified pediatrician in Las Vegas, Nevada. She attended Stanford University, where she received a BA in Human Biology and was the first African American on Stanford University Women's Gymnastics Team. After graduating from Stanford University, she attended medical school at Washington University School of Medicine in St. Louis, Missouri, and completed her internship and residency at Cardinal Glennon Children's Hospital.

Besides being a pediatrician, she competes in fitness and dance competitions. She has competed in over sixty shows over the past twenty years, with many top-place finishes. In 2011, she placed first in Fitness America Classic and in 2019, she was named the AAU 2019 North American Bodybuilding and Fitness Athlete of the Year. In September 2022, she won gold at the Nevada State Senior Olympics, and in June 2024, she competed in the World Fitness Forum and received first place.

In addition to practicing medicine and competing, she became an author in June 2020. During the COVID pandemic, she published her first book entitled *K.I.S.S.: Keep It Short and Simple for a Healthy,*

Sustainable Lifestyle. She bundled all her knowledge as a physician, former collegiate athlete, and fitness professional to create the ultimate guide for living a healthy, yet simple lifestyle. Her second book, *The Sugar Seduction* was published in April of 2022. More recently, she released the first book of a comic book series for children, titled, *The Sugar Attack.* This series will educate our youth about health, nutrition, and wellness with the goal of mitigating some of the chronic diseases we see in adults. During this stage in her life, her goal is to educate the masses through her books and weekly Facebook Live health talks on Tuesday mornings. She has been the guest speaker on many podcasts including Stanford Pathfinders.

She is married to Dr. Carl Allen and has three children and one granddaughter. Her twin sons graduated from Stanford University in June 2017 and were the third set of twins to play for the Stanford Men's Basketball team. One of the twins is currently in medical school and the other twin is in law school. Her daughter is a practicing attorney in Houston, Texas, and her granddaughter just graduated from high school. Dr. Trina continues to be involved with the Stanford community. She is currently the president of the Stanford Club of Southern Nevada.

CHAPTER 6

Rebuilt Strong: Discovering Purpose After Divorce

by Tracy Glass

Most women do not meet their prince charming, plan their fairy tale wedding, stand before witnesses and God, declare unwavering until-death-do-us-part love for their spouse, and then expect their marriage to end. When divorce happens, it can be jarring and conflicting as it goes against the belief of a lifelong commitment.

I made a heartfelt promise: "I will never divorce." But, after twenty-four years of marriage and two children, divorce knocked on my door, sneered at me, and said, "Hello! I'm your new friend." I didn't want to accept the reality of this new relationship. I walked into an unfamiliar new chapter, the only person in my immediate family to face a divorce.

I didn't have a prior perspective on the dos and don'ts of divorce, nor did I have a divorce coach to help guide me through the process. To recover, I would have to come to accept my new normal, and if I didn't take the necessary steps to heal, the pain I experienced might become a life sentence.

It wasn't until nine months after being served with divorce papers that the weight of my new marital status sank in. Despite the chaos swirling around me, I made a conscious effort to stay composed as best as possible. My priority became clear: I needed to navigate this journey successfully to ensure the well-being of both me and my children. Aware of the countless stories of the negative impacts of divorce, I resolved not to become another statistic. I envisioned a future where we would come out of this fire healed. I'm a planner, so I got busy crafting a detailed recovery plan with ten easy steps to overcome divorce's grip and find freedom.

I learned that coming up with easy steps to overcome and heal from divorce was unrealistic. Recovering after a divorce is one of the most challenging emotional battles to face in life. I knew how to clean up children and work messes, but this relational mess stripped away all my problem-solving skills. Unfortunately, this disaster became beyond my expertise to fix. I prayed and asked God, "How are you going to fix my messy life?"

Who is That Girl?

I dreamed of becoming a better version of myself—the 2.0 version where I fully grasped who I was, not just based on my titles or relationship status. I envisioned a girl comfortable and confident in her own skin, one who didn't measure herself against others or merely watch from the sidelines as others showcased their best moments. I wanted to create my own highlights. I prayed to God, asking to become that girl.

As I considered how to reconstruct my life and plan my next moves, I faced a tough question: "Who am I today?" It was crucial for me to explore my values, passions, and purpose. However, there was a challenge; I didn't really know myself. My identity had been confined to being a wife, mother, and employee. It's sad to admit, but it was the reality. Recognizing this, I decided to seek help.

I sought professional help through counseling. My counseling sessions were leading me in the direction of discovering myself and my God-created purpose. The version of me before life's issues and detours got me stuck—the direction of my new and best life.

For so long, my mind was consumed by the negative aspects of my life. It felt nearly impossible to shift my thinking toward something positive, like stepping into my true purpose. I never imagined that the process of healing could happen simultaneously with uncovering a new, meaningful purpose! I finally reached a point where I knew I had to intentionally begin this quest to uncover the calling God had placed on my life. Negativity had been my default for far too long.

I originally thought that the quickest way to find my purpose was to rush toward my destination. But as I progressed, I learned valuable lessons that encouraged me to slow down and appreciate the journey to finding my purpose. I realized to fully embrace life after divorce, I needed to overcome self-imposed barriers, explore new areas, and embrace my uncertainties. This journey has turned into the most enriching, enjoyable, and exhilarating adventure of my life. Here are some insights I've gained along the way:

Breaking Down Walls of Protection

In the aftermath of divorce, I constructed rigid boundaries around my life as a means of self-protection. Any new person or situation needed to pass an internal "boundary test" before being allowed entry. I craved the familiarity of my old routines and habits because they felt safe and comfortable, even if it meant going back to an unhealthy situation. My world had shattered, and sticking to a predictable existence was a way to maintain control and relax my guard.

My rationale: I would never again make myself vulnerable to that level of devastation and pain. If someone or something appeared remotely risky or capable of wounding me further, I would disconnect and exit stage left. Keeping people at arm's length and living within my firmly established confines became my highest priority and kept me safe.

However, I slowly awoke to the fact that these limitations were preventing me from embracing change, exploring new opportunities, and living my best life. Despite craving safety above all else, my self-protectiveness also kept me stuck—stunting my growth and holding me captive in a spiritual and emotional coma.

Boundaries can serve both positive and negative functions. I discovered I needed both to balance my life. Healthy boundaries helped me establish limits, promote self-care, facilitate respect, and create space for stable relationships to flourish. But when my boundaries became negative—unnecessarily restrictive, stemming from past trauma, fear, and self-limiting beliefs—they became personal prisons in my heart, sabotaging my ability to reach my true God-given potential.

I re-evaluated and redefined the boundaries in my life. Simply letting go wasn't the answer; that would leave me unprotected. I needed to find the courage to dismantle the restricting barriers I constructed. They were preventing me from moving forward into the best life God destined for me.

Boundaries or Fear?

I discovered the root of my intense need for safe boundaries: fear. Raw, paralytic fear propelled me to erect walls around my life after my divorce. Fear overpowered me enough to believe that something or someone threatened my well-being. Fear compelled me into self-protection, convincing me to shield myself from potential hurt at all costs. As I stared fear in the face, its constricting power exhausted me and shut me down.

Fear was the enemy preventing my ability to grow, change, embrace joy, and fulfill my purpose. Fear held me back from experiencing life to the fullest by keeping me awake at night and tormenting me. Fear caused me to push away opportunities for loving relationships, punishing myself by remaining isolated. I was trapped in relentless cycles of guilt, shame, and mistrust of others. My fears judged people and convinced me to control every situation to minimize risk.

For a season, this fear had been a survival mechanism, protecting me from further emotional trauma. But soon, my relationship with fear shifted from a shield to a cruel jailer—killing my dreams, keeping me shackled in terror, risk-averse, and insecure. Fear, my greatest obstacle, convinced me to never release control. And without realizing it, I tried controlling God through my prayers, seeking only things that aligned with what I thought was best rather than His perfect plans and purpose. When God showed me this truth, it devastated me.

During a family vacation celebrating my daughter's college graduation, everything became crystal clear. I was reading David G. Benner's book, *Desiring God's Will: Aligning Our Hearts with the Heart of God.* His chapter on willfulness resonated deeply within me. It became evident I was resisting the direction God intended for my life. He stood on the right path, while my controlling fears had me traveling a separate way on the left. God invited me to change directions and join Him, but I was hesitant. My path was known, predictable, and safe. But God's way was risky, unknown, and required me to forfeit control. I realized I had two choices: to either keep doing things my way or to follow God's leading and trust His path.

Embracing a Change in Direction.

I was lost and afraid on the path I was taking. If I didn't make a course correction, I might become permanently lost. In desperation, I chose to leave the safe, familiar path I had been traveling and go where God was leading me, even though His way was unknown. It wasn't an easy shift by any means. As I learned to trust God with my future, I found His strength enabling me to walk through doors that were opening, leading me to heal and to rebuild my life.

The scripture, "I can do all things through Christ who strengthens me" (Philippians 4:13 NKJV), became oxygen to my soul during this season of transition. God was making it clear that my past regrets, failures, and sense of lack were nothing compared to what He was about to do through me. This stripping away of my self-sufficiency was painful but necessary to rebuild me.

Shifting My Perspectives and Mindset

I've realized that my perspective acts as a lens through which I filter all of life's experiences—like a panoramic camera capturing every detail from left to right. My views have shaped my attitude, mindset, opinions, beliefs, and overall perception of reality. Navigating the challenges of a divorce was only one event that shifted my outlook for a season. My childhood experiences have also contributed to forming my viewpoint and have directly impacted the boundaries, internal comfort zones, the fears I face, and my willingness (or unwillingness) to embrace change and take risks.

I cannot erase or change my life's story or complain my way out of problems. However, I can challenge my self-imposed limiting beliefs by adopting a fresh positive mindset; reframing my difficulties as potential opportunities. While honoring my past has been essential for me to heal, it has also been an effective approach for me to lean into a new way forward.

When I decided to surrender to God's direction in life, rather than stubbornly clinging to my own, my divorce perspective shifted in a life-giving way. As I viewed my circumstances through the lens of God's higher vantage point, my fears began to lose their grip. My heart opened to receive the new restorative things He had planned for me in my next chapter, my best chapter.

If my mindset had remained blinded by the bitterness and pain of the past, and stuck in my limited human perspective, why would God have directed me toward the new open doors ahead? If I had refused to make that inner shift, I would have kept going left, walking past the promises and callings God had prepared for me.

From Broken to Beautiful

My divorce represented an ending and a beautiful beginning. It painfully closed one chapter yet sparked a new journey of awareness, healing, and stepping into my God-given purpose. My brokenness made space for God's redemptive work of restoration; remolding me into the woman He created me to be, and me becoming inwardly beautiful again.

The road back to beauty wasn't easy or free of setbacks. There were many days I walked in fear, shame, and the temptation to erect boundaries to stay safe. However, I realized that pain was the fuel I needed to rebuild and realign my mindset through the lens of how God saw me, just as I was. I didn't need to get myself together to start my purpose journey. God's plan was to use me right in my mess, helping me navigate the journey forward. My brokenness had beauty, which gave me renewed courage to press onward.

On my journey of healing and discovering the new me, God taught me a powerful lesson about trusting Him. I realized that the key was letting go of my need to control everything because I was in a loving and safe place with Him. He is always reliable. I didn't need to control everything; I felt His love. I felt safe, and I could relinquish control.

As I prepared to launch my new book *Get Up, Girl, Let's Go: Getting Unstuck and Living Free*, God spoke to me about creating a "miracle challenge" on social media before the book's release. Immediately, fear gripped my heart. I started making excuses why I wasn't the right person for this task. *I need to be more spiritual. Who am I to talk about miracles? I'm certainly no expert. What if no one signs up? What if people judge me?* Doubts and insecurities flooded my mind, and I decided not to move forward with the challenge. It felt like the challenge was too much of a stretch outside my comfort zone. I was paralyzed by fear.

A few days later, I had a dream. I was on a road with Jesus. He asked me, "Why didn't you do the challenge?" I replied, "I was afraid." Jesus led me to a door and asked me to open it. I opened the door and saw hundreds of beautifully wrapped presents. I got excited and asked Jesus, "Are these for me?" He replied, "No, but they could have been if you had obeyed." He also told me the challenge would have increased many people's faith.

After having the powerful dream, I knew I had to move forward with the "miracle challenge" despite being gripped by fear and doubts. I prayed and asked God for fifty people to sign up, hoping that was an attainable goal. Little did I know, God had much bigger plans. When I finally took that leap of faith, God exceeded my expectations in the most incredible way. Over 300 people ended up participating in the challenge! This experience strengthened my faith tremendously and here is what I learned.

Reflections on Resilience

1. God does His best work when I'm not relying on my own intellect or perceived limitations but trusting fully in Him. My role is to stay obedient and have faith, even when it makes no sense to my human understanding.

2. I should never put God in a box by underestimating His power and ability to move in my life. Praying for only fifty signups demonstrated how I had capped the miraculous at a number that was still in my comfort zone. God's ways are higher than our ways.

3. Miracles happen when I partner with God wholeheartedly and act despite my fears. Had I let fear dictate my choices, I would have missed out on this incredible display of God's power and provision.

4. While staying in my comfort zone feels safer, the benefits of taking giant, scary leaps of faith far outweigh the perceived risks. This experience propelled me into deeper levels of trust and dependency on God.

I realized I could never put God in a box again based on my own human logic or experiences. When I finally surrendered control, that's when the real miracles happened beyond my wildest dreams.

People often ask me how I conquered my divorce and found my current purpose. Looking back, if I had to name one thing, it's that I delved deep into understanding myself as a woman and the God who made me. That's when doors to a path far more beautiful than I imagined swung open—a journey to purpose.

Can pain really lead to our purpose? Absolutely, I stand today as a certified life coach, author, speaker, ministry leader, and beacon of hope for women navigating divorce's challenges. I can hardly believe how God has redeemed my rejection and loss and reshaped it into an opportunity to share hope with others traversing similar pain. If someone had told me years ago that this challenging divorce would ultimately unlock my purpose rather than destroy me, I would have said, "I can't believe that." God delights in turning our most challenging times into opportunities of growth.

So, I encourage any woman reading this who feels trapped by past wounds, gripped by fear, or hopelessly stalled on their purpose journey—take heart! No situation is too broken or beyond the reach of God's restorative touch. Be bold and take that first step of acknowledging where you need His empowering strength. Ask Him to shift your mindset and tear down any stubborn walls of self-protection stunting your growth. And get ready, for God will blossom you into the fullness of who you were destined to become.

TRACY GLASS is a powerful testimony to God's restorative promises after experiencing a broken relationship. Eight years after walking through her own divorce, Tracy remarried, her life reflecting the Lord's desire to rebuild what was once shattered. Today, she is dedicated to guiding women toward wholeness and empowering them to wholly embrace their divine identities as God's cherished daughters.

As an award-winning author, sought-after speaker, and certified life coach, Tracy leads a vibrant coaching and mentoring ministry along with a divorce recovery group for women in need of hope and healing. Skillfully weaving biblical truth with personal story, her dynamic teachings and coaching motivate women to deepen their connection with the Lord as the unshakable source of true fulfillment. Through vulnerability and wisdom, she illuminates practical paths for navigating life's obstacles by fixing our eyes on God's superior promises rather than temporal circumstances.

In July 2024, Tracy released her third book, *Restored: God's Promises to Beautifully Rebuild You After Divorce or Separation.* This follows her acclaimed book, *Get Up, Girl, Let's Go: Getting Unstuck and Living Free*, which won the prestigious Golden Scroll Christian Living Book of the Year award in 2022. That book also serves as the companion guide for her 12-week coaching program UNSTUCK: Unlock Your Potential, aimed at inspiring life-changing transformation for women in need of breakthrough.

At her core, Tracy is a cheerleader for the dreams God has deposited in every woman's soul. She enthusiastically advocates for cultivating communities of faith where women can experience God's healing love, safely shed insecurities, and rise into their fullest identity in Christ. Based in the San Francisco Bay Area, Tracy resides with her new husband Joe, their children, and grandson—her greatest legacy being a family redeemed and restored by the unrelenting grace of the Lord she loves. Feel free to contact Tracy at: tracyglasscoaching.com.

CHAPTER 7

Trauma Gets Heavy

by Gail Moody

"It's time to wake up now. Come on sleepy head before you miss the bathroom and then you'll be late for school. Get down those steps and wash your face and brush your teeth so that you don't make yourself late for school and you can't make Donna late because she has to get to school after she drops you off!"

I can still remember my grandmother's words echoing in my head. Little did she know that I was hoping not to have to go to school, and most of all, not to have Donna take me or pick me up. It's hard to fathom how a six-year-old child can process that she is being molested by her babysitter. More importantly, how does that six-year-old know if there is anyone she can trust with that truth who will actually believe her? It has taken many years for that little girl to understand she is not alone.

As an adult, I have come to understand that like myself, there are many children who have been subjected to unbelievable horrors at the hands of adults that have been tasked with their care. My trauma began as a child but it didn't end there. My story is not much different than so many others whose trauma and pain has taken up residence deep within their souls. Not just the molestation, but the death of two people who I loved so deeply. First my grandmother, whose very air I breathed, then my mother who spent much of my life, I believe, regretting that she was unable to provide my sister and I with a safe and stable home. Both died before I reached the age of twelve, which caused me to be passed around from house to house before landing in an environment that would be considered unfit to raise a child by today's standards. These experiences would have been a lot for most adults to process, let alone two children. Yet, I managed to move along, bury the trauma, and take it with me.

Never having received therapy or help for my pain, I continued through middle school and high school carrying the burden and pain of past hurts. I began to get in trouble in school and was labeled a problem child because no one knew nor did they understand what had happened to me. Our prison and mental health facilities are filled with men, women, and children, who have been forced to carry the pains of their past traumas, with no true understanding of how these incidents have affected them, nor how they should go about seeking help to unpack that pain. As a result of my experiences, I often find myself wondering how many kids that we see on the news committing horrific acts who have had to train themselves to be desensitized to their own suffering, thereby making themselves numb to the suffering of others. What may seem to us like insanity or cruelty at the hands of these individuals, may actually be, in their minds, a form of survival.

Thankfully, in high school, I gained some amazing mentors who taught me to channel my pain into things more constructive. What I actually learned though, is how to appear okay and bury the suffering that still haunted me in a deeply subconscious place. That not only helped me to function, it gave others comfort in believing that I was thriving in spite of my trauma. Imagine that...burying your pain so that others won't have to be burdened by the knowledge that you may not be okay. The truth is, trauma will find a way to reveal itself.

As expected, as a young adult, my relationship preferences also displayed my pain. Have you heard the saying, "nice guys finish last!" Well for a woman who has been cut deeply throughout her life without allowing the wounds to heal, that saying is definitely true...or so it was in my case. The more chaos the man could bring, the more I was completely drawn to him. Nice guys never lasted. I married twice, once to a decent and kind man, who is still one of my dearest friends, but whose kindness I could never understand nor appreciate. The other... well let's just say that I stayed for twenty years before God forced me to deal with my trauma. Trauma will tell you that no matter how bad a situation pains you, you deserve to sit in it because you are not worthy of more.

As a wife, I withstood some of the most horrific mental abuse imaginable while creating a fantasy life in the eyes of the public. A life that I so desperately desired, but was never able to attain. What the world was allowed to see was a perfect marriage and a loving husband. That is exactly what I intended for them to see. Much like social media, you create the life and the story that you want people to believe, and I had become a master storyteller.

You see, trauma is like a stain on the rug. It's not going anywhere and will probably get worse and become uglier, the longer you take to address it. Instead, I grew used to the stain and after a while, I barely even noticed that it was there. I learned to compartmentalize that pain and create space for the trauma experiences, allowing them to fit into the space in my brain that I rarely had the courage to visit.

Courage or not, I was forced to face my recent trauma by finding out that my husband of twenty years was having an affair with my neighbor. I finally had to pull back the sofa and deal with the stain in the rug. I woke up one day and realized that the stain was now covering the entire rug. By walking on it every day, without so much as using a sponge or a carpet cleaner on that spot, it had now started to eat through the rug and cause damage so deep in the fiber that it might possibly be too late to repair. So I was finally forced to go and get help.

In spite of the stigma that often comes with therapy, it has helped me to understand how someone could go through years of suffering before ever having a revelation about a need for healing or before reaching a breaking point. Yes, each of us has a breaking point because our capacity for pain absolutely has a limit. The hope is that we identify the needs to heal the scars early enough so as not to bleed all over those who truly care about us.

The difficulty can be that some of us have a higher pain capacity than others, so we advise people to suck it up because someone else did or grin and bear it because someone else who went through it **appears** to have come through it unscathed. We're told that we should just pick up and move on because that's what strong people do. This, my friend, is the true definition of insanity. The idea that therapy is "for white people," (as we are often told in the black community) and that we should just deal with it internally and move on is what makes you truly weak.

The reality is, we all have a limit before which the pain will start to pour out. The pain can pour out in many forms and can even start to cause pain for others around us without us ever intending to. An unhealed soul can raise scarred children or cause damage to a marriage among other things. That is why it's so important that we start to identify and recognize the things from our past that have caused us trauma, which in turn, will spill over into how we live and make life choices every day. Here's why the healing can be difficult: we don't always recognize that we've been so deeply scarred by certain events and that it is destroying our ability to live healthy and prosperous lives.

I personally believe that there are very few women or men who are not in need of some form of therapy to uncover that pain resulting from some form of trauma. Even those who profess to have had the happiest of childhoods and most fulfilled adult lives, will through the rigors of therapy, discover that there are some things that happened to them that they have held onto and continue to make life decisions through that very broken lens. Even if you had the perfect childhood and never had a day of disappointment, that too can create trauma because it has likely placed you in a position not to be prepared to receive the many disappointments that life will surely send your way. For example, we always want to protect our children from pain, but that protection can sometimes be the very thing that hurts them by denying them the ability to develop the much needed coping skills to heal and adapt when life throws them a curveball.

One of the hardest things for many of us to figure out is how to come out of a place of pain and trauma. I am, by no means, presenting myself as a trauma expert. What I am, is a person like many of you, who is working through what it feels like to have normalcy after trauma. What I have realized though, is that I cannot start with today and overlook all of the past trauma that I have suppressed for so long because doing so will allow the trauma to continue to fester. I have to have the courage to have a talk with my younger self about what happened to her.

I need to have a talk with the little girl who was molested by her babysitter at six years old. I need to hug the little girl who was molested by her uncle at seven years old. I need to give a voice to the little girl who was passed from house to house as a child because her parents couldn't raise her. I have to embrace the little girl whose parents split when she was a baby so she only saw her father in passing from time to time. I need to give a warm embrace to the little seven year old girl who is crying out because her grandmother, the one person who showed her unconditional love, went into a coma lying next to her in bed as they watched cartoons and never came out of that coma. I need to cry for the little girl whose mother finally came for her when she was nine years old only to die suddenly by the time she was eleven, making that little girl once again a homeless orphan.

I want to sit her down and let her know that I still love her in spite of all of the bad decisions that I made as an adult from a place of pain. I want to apologize to her for subjecting her to men who I thought she should love and that they would reciprocate that love and not abuse her further, adding to her burdens.

Do you have a little girl in you that needs to hear from you too? What do you need to tell her? It's so easy for others to dismiss her pain, especially for those of us who are viewed as strong. "She's okay! Just leave her alone." "She's young. She'll get over it." "She'll come out of it okay. She's a woman, she was built to handle pain!" These are statements of dismissal that minimize the level of suffering that the little girl has been forced to endure.

I think that for many people, it's just easier to act as if they don't know what you have been through or better yet, that they didn't sit back and watch it happen and do nothing to help. That's not to place blame, sometimes, people don't know what to do, so they do nothing, or convince themselves that they should mind their own business. Others have just been so traumatized by their own situations that they figure since they got through it, so will you. In most cases that's absolutely not the way it works out.

We may get through it, but at what cost? We get through it, but we take that trauma or what I like to call, that bag of rocks with us and it gets heavier and heavier because the damaged little girl continues to make decisions and place her adult self into positions to be traumatized again and again.

You see, damaged people view chaos and pain-permitting practices as normal. What do I mean by pain-permitting practices? I mean that when you have the knowledge and the resources to walk away from or to avoid a bad situation, but you choose to walk straight into it and find a home there.

The damaged little girl gets her energy from being in a bad situation. She feeds on it and unwittingly allows it to create a world around her that is so damaging, yet so familiar, it becomes sadly comforting to her. Why? Because that damaged little girl never leaves us.

She has waited a lifetime for you to acknowledge that she has carried those rocks for you, but she never heard from you. You never acknowledged her pain and told her you were sorry. So she stays with you carrying a weight that she was never meant to bear. So she remains with you, continuing to carry the burden of what you needed her to carry for you; that bag of rocks that she is forced to carry has gotten heavier and heavier. Until one day, the bag becomes too heavy for her to lift, so she drops the bag, and slowly, the rocks begin to fall out. Each rock holds a story, some filled with loss, others with pain we try to ignore. But no matter how long we carry them, we'll never have relief until we decide to put them down.

The molestation rock may cause promiscuity or lack of sexual desire with your partner. The lack of paternal love rock can cause you to desperately hold on to partners, who you are well aware, are damaging to your very soul. The abusive or negligent parent rock can cause you to never, ever feel good enough, which causes you to constantly seek approval and gratification from the wrong people. It's not until you gather the strength to allow God to take the rocks out of your bag, and then get help understanding why you held onto them so long in the first place, that you can truly move forward and find peace. Whether it's through therapy or some other form of counseling, the courage to get the help that you need is the road to healing.

So, what rocks is the little girl carrying for you and how will you help her to unload them? Well, you begin by acknowledging that she was wronged, and that it wasn't that little girl's fault, and you forgive yourself for forcing her to carry that burden for you until you were ready to unload the rocks. You thank her for her courage and for allowing you the time that you needed to carry and release your burdens, be it ever so late. You honor her by doing the work and helping yourself and others to heal so that you are equipped to carry future rocks that may be placed in your emotional bag of life! Get help and get healed queens! That little girl needs all of you to help her unload the heavy burden that she has so bravely carried for you!

Reflections on Resilience

Healing isn't about letting go of the past; it's about understanding why we were holding on so tightly in the first place. Start with a simple step: acknowledge the little girl inside of you. Tell her she is seen, she is loved, and most importantly, she is safe. The weight of your past does not define you. The moment you choose to release it, you step into the life you were meant to live.

GAIL MOODY is a business owner located in Baltimore specializing in providing insurance and financial services. She is a graduate of Morgan State University, one of the premier HBCU's in the country. She is a member of Delta Sigma Theta Sorority, Inc. as well as a member of The National Coalition of 100 Black Women, Metropolitan Baltimore Chapter. Gail is a founding member of the Charlize Angel LaTonya Gilliam Foundation, Inc. which provides scholarships to deserving students in Baltimore. She is the proud mother of two adult children, Stephen and Jordan. Connect with Gail at @gsquad_chronicles on Instagram.

CHAPTER 8

When Does Life Begin?

by Kyra Marshall Walker

I've often asked myself this question and I often wonder, when does life begin?

Does life begin with your first breath, your wail of protest against existence, or the moment of your true awakening?

When does life begin?

When I ask myself this question, I have several answers.

My life began with prayer whispered alongside my name. Lord have mercy. Lord have mercy. Christ have mercy. Lord have mercy. My life almost ended before it began on that unseasonably hot April day in 1976. My life was to end on that day with my mother who was struggling to birth me, and in that instant the ancestors heard her prayer, "Lord have mercy."

From that moment, that brief moment in time, my path was altered, her destiny extended, and she prayed. "Lord have mercy. Christ have mercy. Lord have mercy."

When does life begin? I didn't have a definition of life until life was taken from me. It was Easter in March and like all good Christians we were celebrating Holy Week, the most wonderful and magical time in my life. My life's existence revolved around the circus, the coming of spring, and the celebration of my birth.

On one particular day, things were different. I don't remember much except the yellow and brown pattern on the floor, the orange plastic sofa that was sucking my thighs like starving leaches, and so many people talking. Yet, I couldn't hear or understand anything that was being said. My mother walked into the house through the back door that lead directly into the kitchen. Orange brown yellow. Orange brown yellow, orange brown yellow black. Black cast iron railings, black bar with glass adornment, black glass stove. The diamond shaped mirror with bulging spheres was dancing, reflecting sound and blurs—reflecting reality. Orange brown yellow. Black.

He was gone. My entire existence was gone. My entire life was gone. My rock. My sword. My shield. Gone. What was I going to do without my sole purpose for life? Who was I going to run to? Who was I going to chase after? Who was I going to pine for? Lord have mercy.

The days seemed surreal. I would sit on the toilet, in the powder room that sat in the front foyer, waiting for the door to open. And he wouldn't come. I would sit and wait in the living room, full of plants, feeling the warm sun on my skin from the patio windows in our Spanish style home. I would sit and let the sun warm me until it faded away. And he wouldn't come. I would walk up the stairs with my finger tracing every welded intersection of black cast iron rail. I would walk up and down the stairs, sit on the stairs, walk to the opening of the hallway on the second floor, and get stuck. The reality of life would choke me and not allow me to take another step because I knew he would not be there, and he would not come.

My favorite handmade doll was trapped in that room. Trapped in that silent room where the memory lingered like a shadow. Trapped with the knowledge and memory that she was the last one to see him alive. She was there. Sitting there in the chair with her neatly braided black yarn hair and perfectly painted eyes. She was there in her gingham red and white dress adorned with ribbons and her feet covered in Easter Sunday socks. She was there, slightly smiling, sitting in his plastic covered chair. Recording all of the memories of his last moments. Not yelling, not screaming, and not crying for help. Just there in his presence as he struggled to breathe. Sitting, waiting for the last bit of life to be choked out of him as his heart struggled to push blood through arteries clogged with decades of racism and emasculation, hatred and poverty, and complicated love. As he cried "Lord have mercy," she sat there, not shedding a tear, not making a sound, not even whispering a prayer to the Lord for mercy.

My life began as I sat with my cousin in the funeral home on Pennsylvania Avenue, in Southeast, DC. We sat there on the fifth row close to each other, so close we were breathing the same breath. So close our eyes moved in syncopation and fluttered, fluttered, fluttered. Our eyes never raised high enough to see him. To look at him was to face our reality. That we, at ten and eleven years old, had crossed the threshold into life. We were now living, taking our first breaths, seeing the world for the first time.

"Lord have mercy." We heard the cries of the women that just couldn't believe he was gone. Lord have mercy. We could hear the silent tears of our uncles and cousins that were too masculine to cry out loud. Lord have mercy. I could see my mother out of the side of my eye rocking in her chair on the first row; eyes swollen, tears not falling, standing strong for everyone. Lord have mercy. What is to become of my life? I prayed, *Lord have mercy* ... who was going to shelter me from the world? Lord. Have. Mercy. My life began in that moment, staring at the floor, refusing to move or look up. If I didn't look up, it wouldn't be real. Lord have mercy.

It was Holy Week, Mundy Thursday, and I was given a choice: go to school and attend the Easter egg hunt or go with my entire family of thirty-five cousins, my mother, her five siblings, and my entire community to the place where my life began—Salem Baptist Church on 9th and N Streets Northwest.

I chose to go to the Easter egg hunt. I felt so much joy and relief just being a ten-year-old little brown girl with frizzy straight hair that was flying out of my neatly braided cornrows. I felt free as I laughed, ran, danced, and filled my bucket with pastel-colored plastic orbs full of sugary beans of joy.

The Lord did have mercy on me and freed me from the nightmare of running down the aisle of the church, stumbling on the plush red velvet runner, jumping into the brown polished casket, holding on too tightly to his neck, tearing off his gray-striped suit as my god brothers pulled me away from the empty shell that was everything in the world to me. I saw myself wailing, *Lord have mercy,* over and over and over again until I fell into a blob onto the floor. I saw myself jumping on the casket as they read his last rites, "Ashes to ashes, dust to dust," *Lord have mercy. Christ have mercy. Lord have mercy.* My 100 pound body would have leaped into hole in Laurel Memorial Cemetery refusing to let go.

In that moment, I chose joy—plastic eggs filled with joy, yellow-marshmallow-chicks joy, Cadbury-egg joy, and sugar-filled-paper-crosses joy—exciting and delightful; but short-lived.

The cast iron gate swung in and the heavy bullet proof door opened. I walked through the front door into the foyer of 1103 Bellevue Street Southeast to a reality I could not face. Everyone was there except for him; my savior, my warrior, my protector. They were all there and everyone stared at me as I froze in my bounce and joy of the day and realized I needed the Lord to have mercy and save me from this moment, this day, this beginning of my life. Everything was once again a blur: the people, the colors, the food, the sounds, and the smells. Everything was muffled and blurred. It all went gray, life moved slowly as if I could barely breathe; as if life was not meant to be and nothing was real.

I woke up in a nightmare filled with sexual assault, isolation, unstable friendships, and unexplainable grief. No one ever spoke of the grief, no one ever mentioned the grief. No one ever said to me, it was okay to not be okay. Life moved from vibrant color to gray tones. From sweet melodies to heavy metal. The Lord had taken His mercy from me and I began to believe it never existed.

When does life begin?

My life began January 5, 1996, when the first snowflakes fell from the sky. I prayed for weeks, "Lord have mercy, Christ have mercy." I would go to church and silently cry while the choir sang their stoic proper renditions of Handel's Messiah. I prayed *Lord have mercy* on her soul and release her from the burden of me. It was me. I was her burden. I was the ball and chain dragging her to the bottom of the ocean, slowly drowning, slowing fading, and slowing wilting away. I prayed and prayed and prayed and prayed. And then it happened. It was a Wednesday. I was born on a Wednesday. My grandfather died on a Wednesday, and here again my life was starting over on a Wednesday. In the middle of the day. In the middle of winter. In the middle of hell. Lord have mercy. Her last day home was August 2, 1995, a Wednesday.

Maybe life begins on Wednesday. Maybe life ends on Wednesday. Maybe we are stuck in a constant loop and my loop is Wednesday.

Or maybe life begins on Tuesday, my son was born on a Tuesday. It was a Tuesday at 3:35 a.m. when he was born after twenty-seven hours of active labor. Maybe my life began on June 20, 2006. Maybe on the cusp of summer, on a warm summer day, after a few hours of sleep, maybe that's when my life began. I wanted to see my baby. I wanted to hold my baby. I wanted to nurse my baby. I wanted to do all of the things I had researched, studied, and learned. And they took him away. They took him away to a little bubble. They took him after they told me to not speak too loud, not to over stimulate him with too much touch, not to touch him except with my two fingers. I remember that day; they had him laid out like a little piglet they were ready to roast. There were so many tubes coming out of his body, so many things strapped to him. The beeping was so loud. The machine was so loud. And they took him.

Maybe life begins on a Tuesday. It was the Fourth of July. My body was still raw and bleeding from having given birth two weeks prior. Everything was still fresh. The wounds, the hurt, the pain, everything. I had his father take me to the hospital to visit with him before we went to my cousin's cookout.

When we walked in, all the way to the back of the NICU, all the way behind all of the other babies, he was there; lifeless, as if he were already gone. He was ready to be roasted and served up as a sacrifice. I looked at his monitor, every number that mattered was so low: his pulse, his oxygen, his blood flow, everything. How could this happen? He was doing great the day before! And why are his eyes covered? Why does he have these huge cups on his ears? Why?

We almost lost him on that day, and my life began again. My life began with the grief that I had carried this beautiful, blond-haired, blue-eyed baby inside of me for forty weeks and he was about leave us. My life began while realizing that it was up to me to cry out LORD HAVE MERCY! *Please don't take away my joy before I even experience it!* My life began when I realized that I loved him more than I loved my mother and I would not survive him leaving in such a distressing manner.

When does life begin?

Did my life begin when I was born? When I learned the love of life? When I became a mother? Or when I lost everything I had? When does the Lord show us mercy? Was God showing me mercy when he took my mother when I was nineteen and had to figure out life on my own because my father had no mercy to give? Was the Lord showing me mercy when he kept my baby alive, or was that the intervention of my mother and all of my ancestors refusing to allow me to know that level of heartache and pain?

Or was it on the Wednesday when I went into the doctor for my regular prenatal checkup, and they couldn't find a heartbeat? My third child knew so much pain and suffering, more than I could have ever imagined. He was conceived out of pain, he was conceived out of the necessity to have sex instead of having to physically fight my spouse. He was conceived in a period of torture and hurt and harm and disrespect. And his life ended in the same way.

It was a Wednesday, in June. The end of the school year. My oldest was having many difficulties adjusting to our new life of constant pain and distress. Constant yelling and fighting. A constant struggle to survive the battlefield of waking up. And in his struggles, they sent him home early from school, asked him not to return for the last two days of school. I arrived home to a grown, Silverback hovering over him spit flying with the rag of words that were tearing apart his soul.

I stepped in the middle of the Silverback and the scared little boy and I said, "If you want to fight someone, you are going to have to fight me." And in that moment my life began. When the words, "You and that retarded ass motherfucker can go get your shit and get out of my house right now," were hurled in my face, the Lord showed the only mercy He could toward my sick baby that was struggling to stay alive inside of me. I felt it. I felt him ball up in a knot and stretch out and never move again.

When the doctor was not able to find the heartbeat, it was confirmation of what I already knew. He was gone ... nothing was bringing him back, and he had found his peace with my mother and grandfather. The Lord was showering him with mercy and withholding it from me; no matter how much I cried out *Lord have mercy*. My life began in that moment when he was birthed without a heartbeat, body lifeless, and me being full of grief.

Does your life begin with grief? They say grief is the ultimate display of love. Grief is the burden we bear and the cost we pay for loving. The grief and guilt I have over my third child's death is overwhelming, even seven years later. That grief takes over my entire body and my mind and shutters me into a ball of nothing. That grief is unspeakable. Not at all like the hollowness I felt for decades after my mother died. That gut-wrenching grief of birthing a baby that you cannot love on or see grow. The soul-burning pain of not hearing your baby cry, not seeing him crawl, not hearing his first words, nothing. So when will the Lord show mercy toward me? What more do I have to endure to prove I am worthy of love and peace?

I now realize it was a Wednesday when my ancestors were protecting me from heartbreak and disaster. It was the Wednesday before Thanksgiving. I arrived to the hospital at 5 a.m. prepared to be induced to give birth to my fourth child. And it was a Wednesday when I left the hospital at 7 p.m., frustrated they had cancelled my induction without telling me and I had to get up extra early and not eat the day before. I left that hospital not realizing the Lord was showing me mercy. The Lord did have mercy on me. My fourth child was born on Thanksgiving Day, exactly one year after his older brother was supposed to be born. The Lord was showing His mercy on me by keeping me alive as I listened to the skeleton staff struggle to revive the mother in the next room. The Lord showed His mercy on me in breaking my Wednesday cycle without me realizing the gravity of the birth of my child.

I've lived through a constant loop of Wednesdays. Wednesdays bring life, Wednesdays bring death, Wednesdays bring sorrow, and Wednesdays bring pain. Wednesdays cause me to cry out to the Lord. *Please have mercy on me.* Please. Please. Lord have mercy. Christ have mercy. Lord have mercy.

Wednesday I was born. Wednesday my mother died. Wednesday my third child died. Wednesday my fourth pregnancy was discovered to be ectopic. Wednesday they sent me home and stopped me from birthing my fourth child. Wednesday my sixth pregnancy was terminated in a dilation and curettage (D&C) because it was no longer viable. And it was a Wednesday when I realized when life begins.

When does life begin?

My life finally began on a Wednesday in April when I was driving up the hill reflecting upon my life. In that moment after forty-seven years of being in the realm of life, I realized all of the pain, struggles, and challenges of my life were not tethered to the Wednesdays of the past. My experiences were mine alone, mine to shape, and I was not living my mother's life. I was on my on wave. I was vibrating in my own frequency and in that moment of existence, my life began. I decided I was going to live my life and stop preparing for my death.

Reflections on Resilience

Kyra's narrative asks us to confront a deeply human question: is life defined by our birth, by moments of joy, or by our capacity to endure pain? In her account, Wednesdays become symbolic—intersecting moments of profound grief, rebirth, and revelation. They challenge the reader to consider the cycles that define their own lives. Are we shaped more by beginnings or by the ability to emerge anew after each ending?

The story doesn't shy away from the messiness of existence, from death in its most tangible forms to the intangible loss of innocence. It threads us through a life where survival becomes an act of defiance. Yet, it does more than recount loss; it celebrates the unyielding spark of humanity that clings to hope even in despair. Kyra reminds us that life is as much about the questions we wrestle with as the answers we find.

Perhaps life doesn't begin just once—it begins every time we choose to claim it again. Every Wednesday in this story becomes a potential turning point, a chance for reflection or renewal. So, as you close this chapter, ask yourself: has your life truly begun, and if not, what will it take for you to begin it?

Kyra Marshall Walker is a distinguished professional and a committed community member, known for her extensive contributions and active involvement in various organizations. A Silver Star Member of Alpha Kappa Alpha Sorority, Incorporated, Kyra exemplifies the values of sisterhood and service. She is also an engaged member of Jack and Jill of America, where she contributes to the development and nurturing of African American youth.

Kyra is a proud mother of three exceptional children: Noah Blackston, a budding entrepreneur; Naomi Walker, a rising dance star; and Nicholas Walker, an aspiring linguist. Her dedication to her family is evident in the achievements and aspirations of her children.

Academically, Kyra holds a Bachelor of Science in Agriculture from North Carolina Agricultural and Technical State University (1998) and a Master of Public Administration from Bowie State University (2003). Currently, she is furthering her education at Marymount University, where she is pursuing an EdD in Education Leadership.

Kyra's passion for learning and growth extends beyond the classroom. She is an avid gardener, spending most days throughout the year tending to her garden. Her life's motto, "Every day you are a hero and villain; it just depends on who you ask," reflects her nuanced understanding of life and relationships.

Kyra Marshall Walker's commitment to education, community service, and personal growth makes her a remarkable figure, inspiring those around her to strive for excellence and make a positive impact in their communities.

CHAPTER 9

Proof of Life:
From Wilderness to Green Pastures

by The Rev. Tara Bedeau, J.D.

> *"...and [I] will transform the Valley of Trouble*
> *into a Door of Hope."*
> —Hosea 2:15

Crawling on the pallet of speckled blankets, I hauled myself forward, one knee at a time. I. HAVE. TO. GET. OUT. Hoisting myself to my knees, I slowly pulled in a ragged breath. Reaching upward, I anchored my right elbow on the desk and leaned heavily. I. HAVE. TO. GET. UP. Pushing with all my might, I swiveled right and hit the computer keyboard with my left forefinger. The darkened room immediately brightened. I stared at the pathway illuminated before me and briefly pausing for a renewal of strength, I began typing one keystroke at a time. I. HAVE. TO. GET. IN. Password accepted, a tiny spiral of assent wisped upward within my belly. Hiking myself up unto the chair, I sat, exhaling with desperate relief. With trembling hands, I guided the mouse, tears blurring my vision as I searched for chaplaincy residency programs.

The Lord Is My Shepherd

How had following my Good Shepherd brought me to this place? I COULD NOT believe where I found myself ... for months I had been lying on the floor of this basement room in a swaddle of comforters, in the dark, weeping, praying, worrying and worshiping like crazy, surviving on fig bars and nutritional shakes, unable to leave the room at all.

Imprisoned by mourning, my life had become so untenable I no longer had the energy or the will to face it. Ten years of losses, betrayals, false accusations, abandonment, heartbreak, broken promises, dashed and aborted dreams, and deep disappointments created the perfect climate for a weighty depression, fueled by an excruciating pain, sparked by deep grief and hopelessness. The wilderness of my soul had drained me. While publicly I was successfully operating a business, privately, opening my own mail struck such terror I avoided it for weeks. I wanted off this bus and no more bad news. And I desperately needed the Shepherd who led me here to lead me out. Or had the Divine left me here to die?

He Makes Me Lie Down

Resurrecting a graduation dream buried some fifteen years earlier, I fled to seminary seeking refuge in the obsessive pursuit I had since a child. The urgency was spurred by heartbreaking losses involving my livelihood and reputation; house and motherhood; network and community; and health and well-being, which all occurred simultaneously with yet another economic recession. All I had built had become rubble, and while both a successful business and an organizational leadership role emerged from it, these life collapses, severely rattled my faith and spirit, rendering them almost unrecognizable in their tattered state. In the space of four years, my life had become a wilderness and I needed a fresh start.

In light of my avalanche of Job-like losses, the invitation was clear; "Come Home." At first I resisted, planning to attend seminary elsewhere. Home was complicated; my body sent alarms about the riskiness of such a return. But, my Good Shepherd was on the move. Utterly un-recognizable to me then, this wilderness experience had been deployed to inaugurate a much needed life reboot, to restore the green pastures of my vitality and viability.

The most compatible academic program for my mid-career aspira-tions was in the same locale. So, I limped back home and to seminary, uncertain then of God, myself and my life; hoping this would be the an-swer to both my mid-life and mid-career crises. Looking back, I realize I was being made to lay down. And in keeping with the Divine character of my Good Shepherd, throughout this time I did not lack.

In Green Pastures

Shepherds labor tirelessly to cultivate green pastures, transforming barren terrain into life-giving nourishment. My Good Shepherd was doing the same for my spirit.

He Leads Me Beside the Still Waters; He Restores My Soul

Seminary was a welcome respite from the devastating traumas of the previous four years. My Good Shepherd led me, grief stricken, to the still waters of long sought community through my classes, and restored my soul in the resident mirroring. I was nourished by the scholarship and critical explorations with like-minded individuals. Similarly valued, we engaged with the subjects we as humans face and fear the most; all encapsulated in questions like: What is this most precious gift called life? And how do we engage [with] it, ourselves and each other, as a human experience with conscious awareness? And [how] does the Divine, Mystery, or the Source of it all fit in?

Exploring and wrestling with these questions through the disciplines and frameworks of philosophy, theology, psychology, literature, and art, enthralled me. While confirming the passion and intelligence for a calling long archived, the process validated the steadfastness of a love thought long disintegrated. Now expansively oriented spiritually and acutely individuated psychologically, I rose to meet my program's rigorous demands while plowing through my grief. As a bonus, I met cultural and vocational kin throughout the city. It appeared that despite the thorny catalysts and financial sacrifice, returning to seminary was a good choice. Hope began to emerge in my breast and my buried plans began to revive.

He Guides Me Along the Right Paths

Sometimes our right paths will take us in the direction of our triggers and traumas so they can be healed, or else they can take over as shepherds. And because trauma stimuli can distort the rightness of a pathway, it is imperative to remain attuned to the Good Shepherd's leading and remember safety is found in trusting the accuracy of His leading.

While seminary proved the right path for my soul restoration, its still waters were located in unpalatable places. It had been more than twenty years since I had lived at home and I was gratefully relieved by the offered hospitality to support my unexpected mid-life career change. Yet, my dormant hopes of it being a different place, most likely activated by my vulnerability, were proven unreasonable during this time of returning.

The ensuing grief was indescribable yet effective: I was empowered to judiciously comprehend the contours of the character—and constraints—of my childhood caregivers, and relate accordingly—with unrestrained maturity. With this liberating truth, I was brought into right relationship, not only with my family, but with my lineage/ancestry and, consequently, myself. This was a key development of my green pastures; featuring the hallmark fragrance of Divine healing.

The "right path" contains rites of passage in pursuit of what is life-giving, which is the chief expression of the Good Shepherd's love and leading. Therefore, when we agree to follow the Good Shepherd, the paths of righteousness upon which we are led are encoded as pathways of healing and wholeness. Now that my right paths, career and home wise, were affirmed, the Good Shepherd was after my identity.

...Even Though I Walk Through the Valley of the Shadow of Death, I Will Fear No Evil [Disaster, Danger or Harm]

As seminary drew to a close, my right paths moved on from still waters. Due to an urgent hip surgery, graduating took a year longer than planned, and despite my best efforts, my post seminary plans were dashed. Instead, I entered what I called my V.S.D (*Valley of the Shadow of Death*), a thirty-month fellowship program, which included two successive surgeries (and promises of an inevitable dual hip replacement); temporary paralysis of a limb; a humiliating reset of my financial house, and the threat of ocular lymphoma with the pressing medical summons for yet another surgical procedure.

While my Good Shepherd did not abandon me during this time, I was stupefied by these new hurdles and losses as I thought the Valley route was behind me. Contrary to the Psalmist, I was afraid ... terrified, enraged, and worn out. Given all I had undergone, how could I "fear no evil?" That is EXACTLY what painful trauma does ... it causes one to fear evil—also translated as disaster, harm or danger. And yet this was the next step in my wilderness to green pastures program; and I was not alone, my Good Shepherd was with me.

The crush of the wilderness experience can make it easy to forget that the challenges experienced are the result of the Good Shepherd's leading and not one's defiance. Right-path walking will bring shadows because they only emerge in the presence of light. And because shadows contain whatever we have hidden, events that conduct their illumination speak to the Good Shepherd's presence. Life's "deaths" in particular, cast large shadows, temporarily blinding one to the rightness of one's path. Yet, in order for the Good Shepherd to create green pastures from our wilderness experiences, we have to address whatever we hid or hoped for in the pre-wilderness journey. A sign of our trust in the process, we have to heal the reveal. And this is no easy task.

No shepherd boy here. I incarnated as an able-bodied, first-generation Caribbean-American, black female. And the deaths I underwent revealed my fears of isolation and aloneness, poverty, chronic health challenges, and entrapment in life-defeating cycles animated by childhood, developmental, familial and generational lineage, culture, and societal dynamics. In short, everything I was afraid would happen did. And I was ashamed.

Most importantly, I was *terrified* of anything more. So overcome by this unrelenting life tsunami, my resiliency was threadbare after ten years of stripping. This amount of suffering exceeded my banks. I was afraid my ability to function would expire, leaving me incapable of building the life of fulfillment I so desired.

Buried within these shadows of my deaths were my deep archetypal senses of being both an orphan and outcast. Belonging to no one, and rejected by all, how loveable could I be and how would I survive this life—much less be content? Furthermore, according to societal norms and social scientific theorems, I was at a great disadvantage, doomed to a life of evil (which is *live* spelled backwards; its opposite).

The enormity of the realities of my situation, the attendant truths, as well as what it would take to fix it, overtook me. Hitting a wall, I took to lying on the basement floor, lost within an engulfing cloud of despair, hopelessness, and blindness. I was in the Valley.

Drowning in the tidal pool of depression in light of this bleak horizon of nothingness, I did the only thing I knew to do. *Worship.* Whatever my fears, whatever the shadows, they were not stronger than my incarnated instinct to seek my Good Shepherd.

For You Are With Me [&] Comfort Me ...
In the Presence of My Enemies

And the chords of our song would play in that dark room, reminding me our connection was older than time. The Divine Presence would descend and instantly my heart would spring forth to meet my Beloved. I would feel the Spirit of the Holy infusing every cell: soothing my heart, grounding my mind, healing my body, reorienting my soul, and bolstering my spirit. And my faith arose anew, as I remembered, time and time again, night after night, hour after hour, minute after minute, praying and weeping in that Gethsemane of a basement room. And I took refuge in the Divine Love. It was a holy communion of mutuality and commitment. And the being that had been lying curled on the blanketed floor, cradled in the dark, soundproof makeshift manger, would ascend, drawing strength and sustenance from the Living Water. Quickened, I would regain my footing as a Holy Priesthood to face another day of wilderness walking.

The Shepherd's comfort, essential for wilderness walking comes through worship, which instills the knowing of the Divine Presence. This engenders fearlessness in the face of evil, which manifests as a tensile strength when enemies threaten to overtake you. Such trust is especially forged via *the right path* of death shadow work when walking in the wilderness valleys.

There, my most formidable enemy awaited. Lurking in the shadow of my deaths was a creeping suicide ideation that haunted me; a reasonable response to the vision-draining, will-sucking, ambition-robbing result of the hopelessness of deep grief and the crippling depression it rode on. Although I did not want to die, I could not keep living like this. Impervious to various self-help and spiritual practices, including medication and inspirational messages, this saboteur was the most powerful enemy I had yet faced. So depleted, *I did not recognize myself.* I was in my hardest battle ... for my will to keep fighting and to live. I am so thankful for my therapist, an agent of my Good Shepherd, who sat Shiva with me and kept faith and sight when I was forlorn and vision-less.

Proverbially stripped to the bone, I dwelled in the gateway between death and revival. It is true, without a vision and hope, one can perish. And I surrendered all of this to my Good Shepherd, who was organizing me and my life.

The Divine was not appalled, surprised, dismayed, or angry by my response or reaction to His leading or its outcome. He had already known what had been hidden to me; the light of His Presence that revealed it! Empowered by the love of the Good Shepherd, my healing required facing these shadows, belief systems, and enemies. The awareness of this made our time together even sweeter and the Divine Love all the more real. And I *understood* that my Good Shepherd was with me, even in the midst of my rage, anguish, shame, terror, and deep exhaustion, as I lay on the basement floor.

Enemies are designed to make you feel separated from the Divine, which is the source of life itself. Thankfully, they always surrender to the Divine Presence: so, I continued to worship my way through.

You Anoint My Head With Oil, My Cup Overflows

Because oil enables the sheep to live victoriously in their environment, their heads are anointed to provide protection, heal wounds and facilitate respiration (oil prevents overheating). And my Good Shepherd did just that.

This lengthy dark night of the soul, became a spiritually fertile time. During that time, I learned I was more than my health, finances, family, career, culture, or social identities; even my own dreams and ambitions. My Good Shepherd mended my orphan and outcast wounds. I was loved and affirmed as a powerful spiritual warrior, teacher, and healer called to walk closely via a joyous, adventurous, and creative contemplative spiritual life. In His presence, revelations were gifted, healings and wonders occurred, chords were broken, soul wounds were healed, generational ills transmuted, and sanity re-tethered. The most significant miracle of all: I was anointed to be able to get up from my basement bed and walk.

Empowered with a visionary unction, my wilderness period drew to a close as I applied for chaplaincy residencies. My green pastures awaited, ironically located in the place I left six years prior: a place that had hurt me so much that I had sworn never to return. But My Good Shepherd was on the move (pattern, anyone?). As the years unfolded, that valley of sorrow and suffering became a door of hope and my former wilderness became green pastures. Ten years after starting seminary, my ordination arrived, yet another vision that had been seeded twenty-five years earlier. Goodness and Mercy continue to be my rearguard and protection.

Surely Goodness and Mercy Shall Follow Me All the Days of My Life

Due to deep grief and pain, I almost died in the wilderness. It was beyond my mind, it was a depression of my entire being. The onslaught of the catastrophes had drained the vitality out of me. Many did not or could not understand. Some thought I did not know or walk with the Good Shepherd. Others considered my troubles overwhelming, contagious, deserved punishment or otherwise warranted, and distanced themselves accordingly. Few recognized I was a fellow sheep. It was a very lonely time ... which drew me closer to my Good Shepherd.

Thanks to His pastoral care, my wilderness years led to greener pastures, ushering me to still waters and a door of hope: the restoration of [a vision for] my career, my community, my creativity, my faith in and care for myself, and deeper intimacy with my God. Most importantly, I live at a firmer place of rest than ever before, thanks to a richer understanding and experience of God's love. This leads to a restful knowing that my life is trustworthy, in all of its unfolding, because my Good Shepherd is with me.

Reflections on Resilience

Tara Bedeau's story is a profound meditation on survival, transformation, and trust in divine guidance through life's most barren landscapes. She invites us to consider the nature of suffering—not as punishment, but as preparation for renewal. The wilderness, she shows us, is not merely a place of loss but of deep excavation, revealing the hidden wounds and fears that must be healed for true restoration.

Her journey underscores a powerful truth: the presence of light is what casts shadows, and it is in those shadows that we confront the essence of our struggles. This confrontation—though terrifying—leads us to the Good Shepherd's care, where we can begin the painstaking process of transformation. Bedeau's experience reminds us that despair and faith can coexist, and in those moments, worship becomes an act of defiance against hopelessness.

Through her narrative, we are prompted to ask ourselves: what is the wilderness teaching us? Are we willing to sit with our shadows, trusting that they will lead to still waters and green pastures? And when we emerge from our valleys, can we embrace life with the renewed faith that even our darkest days serve a higher purpose?

THE REV. TARA BEDEAU, J.D., is the Founder and Principal of Walking the Wisdom Way. It supports people seeking to engage life with intention, skillful wisdom, and conscious awareness —from a place of love (goodwill) and truth and not fear. As a Speaker, Author, Coach, Consultant, and Educator, she mentors and guides people in identifying what is most life giving, in support of their wholeness, goal attainment, and human flourishing.

The Rev. Bedeau draws on decades of experience and education as an Attorney and Executive Leader; Executive, Wisdom and Life Coach; Chaplain and Spiritual Director; and Fellow Seeker, specializing in the integration of Psychology and Spiritual Care; Equity, Inclusion and Belonging; US Employment Law; Leadership and Organizational Development and Change Management. The Rev. Bedeau has traveled and lived throughout the globe, learning and participating in wisdom and wellness communities. Collectively, clients include emotionally intelligent seekers, leaders, culture shifters, and change agents. She can be reached at www.thepreciseaim.com/wisdom.

CHAPTER 10

What Do You Do When You Don't Know What To Do?

by Dr. Terri Hackett

"There are two loves in life, what you do and who you do it with."
Soul Food (Series)

I am married! I was so excited to be a wife, I had finally found my best friend and we married each other. Our love story was both simple and complex. We met because he owned a cheesesteak restaurant with my friend Joe, whom I had a small tiff with. I went to the "shop" (that is what we called it) to find him. Troy was there and told me Joe wasn't there. That is how we met. He was cute but not my focus at the moment.

Fast forward to a couple of weeks later and my friend Leslie called me on a Saturday morning and said, "Guess who likes you?!" I was like *that is so high school*.... But who?? She told me Troy from the shop kept asking about me. So, I found myself eating a lot of chicken cheesesteak sandwiches and even made my school order them for the teachers. We finally went on our first date to the movies and the rest is history.

I had been married eleven months, but that summer, both of us were working so hard we barely saw each other. We worked opposite hours.

I was at the community college working days and he was working evenings and closing the shop each night. The day before my life changed, Troy came home early, and we were sitting on the porch talking. He was telling me how hard things were and he and his partners were determined to make it work. We talked about how he knew God would take care of him and we would see the other side. I told him I believed in him, and I would always be there supporting him. The next day we talked, and he said he would be home after he closed. I told him I loved him, and he told me he loved me. I went to bed.

I woke up the next morning and Troy wasn't there. Strange ... I called, no answer. I called, no answer. I called. Now I am mad. *Who do you think you are staying out with all night?* I thought. I went to the gym and came home and still, no answer.

At this point, anger turned into concern. I called my friend and Troy's business partner. We called the hospitals, but he wasn't at any of them—what a relief. We then called a police officer who was a friend, and he started the process of officially looking for Troy.

In the meantime, someone called and told me they saw Troy's car on the news and there had been a shooting. I didn't believe any of it. My friends convinced me to go to the morgue. I went, but refused to go in. My friends went inside, and they found him. Troy had been robbed, shot, and killed on his way to deposit the night's money. A single bullet shattered my world.

After two funerals, one in Seattle and one in Philadelphia, I was spent. Alone, I went back home to the house we lived in. Our outside stairs were hollow, and you could hear the echoes from footsteps coming up the stairs. For weeks, I sat in silence straining to hear Troy's familiar steps on those hollow stairs, knowing deep down

I never would. I tried so hard to move on, go back to work, be normal, but it was hard.

I attended church my whole life and was very active from an early age. I thought I was saved and knew the Lord, but when this happened, I realized that I didn't know Him as well as I thought. I needed Him now more than ever. I prayed and prayed for God to help me get up each morning and go to sleep each night. I prayed He would help me make it through each day and take the pain away. In the depths of my despair, God's presence was steadfast, comforting me when I felt most alone.

I had wonderful family and friends who supported me, encouraged me, and convinced me I needed to go to grief counseling, which was really helpful. I no longer felt I was losing my mind each day, (just some days). But I needed more.

When I went back to work after the funeral, a new boss was in place. She was horrible to me. She was unkind, unreasonable, and unsympathetic to my situation. I found a coping mechanism in travel. When I traveled, I didn't have to think, I just had to enjoy. I took a cruise and visited friends and family all over the country.

One of my travels led me to Missouri; a close friend had recently received his new church appointment and invited me to his friends and family Sunday service. There I met his best friend and fiancée at the time, and we just hit it off. I often say that when she and I walked into the Coach store together, she understood. Our friendship was sealed. By the end of the weekend, plans were made for me to visit them in Maryland for Memorial Day. That set off a chain of events that led me to where I am today.

I visited my new friends, and I wound up coordinating their wedding. In that year I visited them at least four times. Troy had been gone two years, and I wasn't really getting any better. Most of my life I had been identified as "Judge Johnson's daughter." When Troy died, I was now identified as "Troy's widow." I so desperately wanted to be "Dr. Terri." My job was getting worse. I learned firsthand how toxic work environments can weigh on both mind and body. I didn't know what to do.

One day I was on the phone with my new friend in Maryland, crying about how horrible life was. She said, "No more! Put your stuff in storage and move in with Mike and me." I told her I wish I could, but they had just married and didn't need me around. Mike took the phone and said, "What Angie said," I thought about it ... I longed to shed the labels and just rediscover Terri, free from expectations. I wanted to be anonymous. I would have to step out on faith. I didn't have a job lined up, but I had savings, and I knew my parents would support me. So, I decided to go for it. I went to my parents and told them my plan, which was hard because in my family you don't do this kind of thing. Surprisingly, they supported me. My father asked me if I was sure I wanted to do this, and my mother cried and said she just wanted me to be happy again.

I put my stuff in storage, shipped my car and the rest of my items, and set out for Gaithersburg, Maryland from Seattle, Washington. I arrived at the end of January and settled in. As I started looking for a job, a friend called and asked me if I would come to Bennett College in North Carolina to work as a Resident Director from February to August. I took the job, but I had to drive to Greensboro, NC, almost six hours away. I had never driven that distance before and was worried I couldn't make it, would fall asleep and run off the road, or I wouldn't know where I was going. All my friends encouraged me. They told me it was just six CDs. If I listened to six CDs, I would be there by the time they were finished.

So, I set out on a snowy February morning; I didn't know how to drive in snow either, but I thought *let's go with it.* As I continued to drive, the snow melted and I felt more comfortable. This was in the early days of cell phones and for most of the trip, mine worked fine. But then it didn't, and I didn't know why. My friend told me to call at a certain point and she would direct me, but now I couldn't. I used common sense, got off, and asked for directions three times, and with God guiding me, I finally made it to Bennett College. When I walked in the door my friend burst into tears; she had no idea what was going on. We discovered that my signal got stuck on a cell tower and it took a week for them to get it off.

I knew my time at Bennett was temporary and I still needed to find a job in Maryland. I went to a conference and attended a session about teaching young African Americans about college access. A grant had been written to provide this service in Baltimore, Maryland. I spoke with the presenter after the session and shared I was looking for a job. She told me she could not afford me because I had a PhD. I emailed her every week for six weeks until she said I could come and interview. That meant another round trip to Maryland. This time I was much better. I interviewed and got the job.

Once I finished my assignment at Bennett, I drove back to Maryland to start my new job. During that time, I met new people, made new friends, and found a church home. But it wasn't without some bumps in the road. Before I made those friends, I was lonely, I thought I wanted anonymity, but I did not realize it meant no one would be around to talk to. After all the time I spent in church knowing everyone and participating, I now struggled to find a church home where I felt comfortable.

But God. My friend, whose church I visited in Missouri, had moved to Maryland before me, and I cried to him about not being able to find a church home. He took me to a church in a high school. The minister was one of my distant mentees from back in the day. When I walked in, I knew I had found my church. In the high school, it was hot in the summer and freezing in the winter, but we made it through. There I met many people and made friends I never knew I couldn't live without. I worked in the church, and slowly but surely, after a several years I was feeling like myself again.

There are days when I often tell people, "I am not supposed to know you" because I am supposed to be married for almost twenty years with a couple of kids and still working at the community college. Instead, I have worked at three Historically Black Colleges and Universities (HBCUs) where I have impacted the lives of amazing African American young people all over the country. I worked for a grant-funded program that specialized in college preparation where I was allowed to create an amazing program for underserved high school students. Now I work at an education non-profit where I help to close the equity gap of students of color and low income students by encouraging them to take more rigorous courses. Working with, supporting, and loving young African-American people has been my lifeline. Serving my community has kept me sane and moving forward. I discovered more than I already knew: this is my calling. When people ask me *why are you on this earth? What is your purpose?* I can answer that question with ease, "To affect the lives of others and learn from them along the way."

I have an awesome church. We moved out of the high school into a bigger space and finally built a church in the DC, Maryland, Virginia area. It has been so exciting, and I am grateful for my spiritual growth, and my pastor and his family for supporting and loving me. I am no longer anonymous, I have wonderful friends here now. People are loving and kind and stand by me no matter what. It is still hard some days and always bittersweet even after all these years. I think of Troy all the time. He would be so happy the Eagles won the Super Bowl and proud that the cheesesteak restaurant is still thriving, and his partners are doing well.

As I share my story, I want people to know that resiliency is real. I never in a million years thought my life would turn out this way, but it has and that is okay. After all these years I am ready to find love again. Some days that is a scary thought; other days, there is a true longing for companionship. I have been out of the dating game for so long, I don't know what to do. Online dating is the devil, and I am too old to go out clubbing anymore. I believe I can find someone who will love me as deeply as I am ready to love them. Maybe there is another best friend out there for me, who knows?

There are so many stories I could tell, so many things I could share, but I think the point has been made. With God by my side, and my own inner strength, in the words of Miss Celie in *The Color Purple,* "I'M HERE!"[1]

Reflections on Resilience

This story is a heartfelt exploration of love, loss, and resilience. It shows us that life often takes us down unexpected paths, testing our strength and challenging our faith. In the midst of grief, Terri found herself grappling with the unthinkable: a life without the future she had envisioned. Yet, her journey reveals the profound truth that even in our darkest moments, there is a light guiding us forward.

---

1   https://www.imdb.com/title/tt0088939/characters/nm0000155

Through faith, community, and an unyielding inner strength, Terri rebuilt her life piece by piece. Her story is a testament to the power of relationships—both human and divine—in shaping our ability to heal and grow. Whether it was the embrace of a new church family or the solace of long-held friendships, she found the support she needed to rediscover herself and her calling.

Terri's journey inspires us to reflect: how do we respond when life disrupts our plans? Can we trust the process, even when the way forward is unclear? And most importantly, can we open ourselves to new possibilities, knowing that life has a way of transforming pain into purpose? Her story reminds us that with faith and determination, we can weather life's storms and emerge stronger, ready to embrace new beginnings.

DR. TERRI HACKETT is a Partnership Director at Equal Opportunity Schools (EOS). Prior to working at EOS, Terri was the Student Ombudsman/Title IX Coordinator at Alabama State University, in Montgomery, Alabama. She served as the chief advocate for students in a confidential environment, supporting their successes as they navigated collegiate responsibilities in pursuit of their degrees. Previously, Terri directed intensive, targeted support to all 1,300 students in the College of Health Professions at Coppin State University in Baltimore, Maryland, where she ensured a seamless transition of recruited students into the Nursing and Allied Health Programs.

Terri's entire career has been based on advocacy and support of students of color in general, and HBCUs specifically. She believes all students can attend college and be successful if they are provided the tools they need.

Terri has Bachelor of Arts in English from Spelman College, a Master of Arts in Education from the University of Central Oklahoma and a PhD in Higher Education Administration from The University of Texas at Austin.

Terri currently resides in Laurel, Maryland, where she is very active in her church Kingdom Fellowship AME Church, The Links Incorporated, and Delta Sigma Theta Sorority, Incorporated. She enjoys cooking, travel, and continually working on her fitness journey.

CHAPTER 11

The Bride Who Wore Black:
Finding God in the Midst of the Storm

by Muriel Evans, MS, PI

The noise seemed distant. I don't know what snapped me out of it—was it the feel of someone pulling me, was it the smoke surrounding me, was it the odd feeling that I was holding something, or was it the sound of a baby crying in the distance? I was slowly coming out of my darkness. My eyes were starting to focus … Oh no! The smoke was coming from the television I had destroyed. The screaming baby was my infant that I'd left by the elevator; that feeling like I was holding something was my arms around her neck. The pulling sensation was my husband's desperate attempt to stop me from choking her. Yes her, the woman I caught him in bed with. I was quiet. I wanted to drop everything and run to sooth my crying baby, but the urge to snap this woman's neck was far greater. What am I doing, how did I let it get to this?

Three Years Earlier

I opened my eyes as the sun filled the room. He was already up getting dressed. I closed my eyes and reminisced about the night before.

The love making, the long passionate kiss afterwards. Damn I loved this man. He came to kiss me before heading out. Didn't even care that I hadn't brushed my teeth as he put his arms around me and stuck his tongue in my mouth. I shivered as he pulled away and said, "What are you going to do today?" I stared at him and thought for a minute and simply said, "I don't know yet."

He smiled and said, "I signed you up for golf lessons at nine, so you need to get up." I thought to myself, *I do not want to play golf* as I watched him wiping his clubs down. He said, "I called the concierge and made a dinner reservation for six. I should be back by then." I smiled as he walked out.

Hopping in the shower, I realized I forgot to call my mother, a routine we started when I was in college. A quick conversation just us girls. While drying off, I picked up the phone in the room and dialed my parents' number. My mother answered on the first ring. She asked what I would be doing today and I explained he had signed me up for golf lessons. I waited for the response she always said when it came to him: "Don't forget whose child you are." I never questioned, but I knew it had some hidden meaning. My thoughts kept yelling HERE I AM MOMMY, spending a week at a five-star resort with a man that makes me laugh, treats me like a queen, and gives me good love. But I kept my mouth shut and wondered, "*What does she know that I don't?*" Hanging up, I noticed a cute, but conservative golf outfit he had left on the chair. Hearing his voice as I put it on and argued, "*Why can't I wear shorts and a halter top?*" He would say, "There is golf etiquette."

Later that day I signed in for my lessons, and although bored, I smiled the entire time. The instructor told me I was a natural. Whatever, golf is not my thing. I decided to go lay by the pool because I knew he would be playing until 6 p.m. It was still early, and I found myself missing him and yearning to be in his presence.

I ordered some food and champagne. My mind wandered thinking about how we met two months prior at a basketball tournament in North Carolina. We exchanged numbers and talked on the phone for two hours every night. I recorded every conversation we had because they were so delightful. We finally agreed he could come to visit me in Rhode Island. I was so excited. We spent one full day and one night together, when all of a sudden his pagers, cell phone, and everything were blowing up.

He turned to me and said, "I have to leave. I need to go to Arizona."

My heart cracked. As he made his travel arrangements, we packed my car and I drove him to the airport. We held hands as I changed gears. We never spoke. After the last twenty-four hours we had just spent together, I knew his needing to go to Arizona was more important than me. When we arrived to the airport, I noticed a few people staring but I didn't care. I was trying to get a hold on what I was feeling. I had never experienced this feeling before.

As he walked up to the counter to purchase his seat on the next flight, I walked over to the window to stare at the planes taking off. I remember like it was yesterday that I closed my eyes and prayed, "My father in heaven, I just want to thank you! If this man NEVER calls me again, I will be fine. Thank you for allowing me to have the best time of my life for these past twenty-four hours." My eyes watered a little as he came up behind me and asked if I was okay. I smiled as he boarded.

I went home that evening, poured a glass of wine, and tried to relax. I had never felt like this before. My feelings were everywhere. Around midnight, my phone started to ring, and I answered. It was him.

"I need to talk to you. Meet me in Florida."

I told him no because I didn't have the money. After he called me three more times to convince me, I finally said yes.

At 7:30 the next morning I had a courier at my door with first class tickets to Florida. It was Sunday. My flight left at two o'clock. During this time, I worked for the governor of Rhode Island. I had to call my office the first thing Monday and take personal leave. I called to tell my mother, and she was quiet.

Waking up, I realized it was only 3:00 p.m., so I walked through the resort and found a hair salon. I thought it would be a good thing to get my hair done. I was the only one in the shop so I taught the Dominican owner how to wrap my hair. As we were talking and drinking champagne, she said, "Your boyfriend is very rich?" I shared with her my story and told her I was nervous because my phone calls from the room were over $300 and I didn't have it.

She said to me, "Tell him you want him to pay for your use of the phone. If he cares for you, he will say, 'Don't worry about it. But you have to ask.'"

She was right.

After he returned from playing eighteen holes, he showered, and we got dressed for dinner, I put on a form fitting white dress with nothing on underneath, and I mean nothing. During dinner he appeared nervous. If I had to get up and use the restroom, he wanted to go. When we stopped to take pictures he had to place his hands over my knees. While we were waiting for our driver, he had to be close to me. He was so worried that someone was going to see what was under my dress that it was comical, so I took advantage of that.

When we returned to the room and started to become very intimate, he stopped and said, "I need to talk to you." He said, "I don't think you know who I am. I play football."

I looked at him and said, "As in the NFL?"

He confirmed. Then it hit me; that's what my mother knew.

So, I kissed him and said, "Let's enjoy each other and when we get to the airport to go home, we will go our separate ways. I don't date professional athletes because I know how they treat women."

At that moment, he fell to his knees, confessing he was falling in love and pleading with me not to leave. I was breathless. That sudden departure from Rhode Island now made sense. He had an offer to sign a major deal with another football team. It was all over the news.

Four Years Later

My life was full of meeting my athlete here or meeting him there. One thing I knew for sure, he was the love of my life. I had never felt like that before. But I was getting pressure from my parents about marriage and other things.

I had convinced my athlete to go with me to Martha's Vineyard and purchase a home that we could rent to earn money. He was excited about it and I had done so much of the research that the realtor was going to allow us to come and stay in the house for a week—rent free. We were so excited. Two days before leaving for the Vineyard, my athlete called me and said he was with his tax attorney, and it didn't look good and we needed to reschedule our trip. I was devastated but had to be understanding. My girlfriend called me and dragged me out of the house to hang out. I had an attitude.

While hanging out with my girlfriend that evening, I met my future husband. He was an attorney, member of the fraternity that was hosting the event, and a smart and funny guy. Because he was a part of the fraternity's leadership, he asked if I could escort him for the weekend. I did.

Six weeks later, he proposed. Although I was in love with my athlete, I said yes, believing I was choosing stability over uncertainty. However, not long after we married I realized the very thing I was running from in my athlete, I got in my marriage—many women and months of infidelity. I learned this man that proposed after knowing me for six weeks had never been faithful in any of his previous relationships. One of his affairs had resulted in a child.

Here I was after an expensive wedding that made my father happy. I stood there full of smiles and laughter taking the vows, but the minute my pastor said. "You are now Mr. and Mrs...." I knew I had made a mistake. I was still in love with my athlete, but how could I tell him what I had done.

I returned to Rhode Island (RI) after my honeymoon. My husband and I agreed, I would fly to and from DC to RI every weekend. After returning to RI from my honeymoon, my athlete had left over ten messages. His team was in the finals to play the Patriots to go to the Super Bowl. My heart stopped. What had I done?

Introducing Mrs.

I settled into being a wife. My husband had a hot meal every time he came home from work. He had breakfast every morning, and I made his lunch and then headed to the office. He sometimes didn't get home until late, and that was fine.

One day I called in sick; I was watching the Oprah show and she had a team of private detectives on that day. I sat and watched as they discussed the top fifteen signs your significant other was cheating on you. I could hear my heart beating. My husband had the first twelve. I wrote the name and number of the detective agency and began to think.

The next day, I called their office and spoke to one of the detectives. The first thing he told me to do was put fresh batteries in my husband's beeper. That night as he slept, I changed the batteries. A few days later, I tried three times to contact him. When he came home that night, I told him I paged you today.

He said, "My batteries are probably dead."

I called the detectives the next day and gave them a credit card. I had married a liar and a cheat. I had to think about my next move, but I kept coming back to one thing: I wanted a child so I had to stay put.

Present Day

As I slowly began to release my hold around her neck, I looked over at him and thought *I gave up everything for you.* We had just built and moved into our home where he promised to make me happy. He promised me I would have everything I wanted. He promised me a life of total bliss. I didn't want to be with him, but I believed his promises of happiness. They were all lies. He lied. Everything about us was a lie. I stepped over the mess I made to calm my screaming baby.

How did I get here? I had no one to talk to. My mother had passed when I was three months pregnant. My brothers were in New England and would probably want to kill him. I had relocated here so my closest friends were wives of his friends. As I was alone and making that drive home that night, I thought how easy it would be to just drive me and my baby over a bridge or into my garage and leave the car running. I had deep thoughts of suicide and was in trouble with no one to turn to. The tears just ran down my face as I drove home trying to decide how I would end it all.

Then I felt it, a calm, a peace that enveloped me like a protective embrace. It felt like someone was holding me. I stopped crying and I knew before I could say it out loud, it was God. He was carrying me. The next morning, I retained an attorney.

I sued my husband for a divorce based on adultery and won. How? As providence would have it, while we were waiting for our court dates for divorce, another woman had his baby which proved adultery.

Reflections on Resilience

Muriel Evans' story is a searing testimony to the power of resilience and the grace of divine intervention. She begins her journey consumed by betrayal and rage, her life unraveling under the weight of broken promises and infidelity. Yet, through her raw account, she reveals a profound truth: even in the depths of despair, there is a path toward healing.

Her narrative forces us to confront the cost of choosing what feels safe over what feels right. As Muriel wrestles with her decisions, we are reminded of the complexity of love, trust, and self-worth. It is in her darkest hour, contemplating the unthinkable, that she finds the calm and presence of God, gently guiding her back to hope and agency.

This chapter challenges readers to reflect: how do we reclaim ourselves after devastation? Can we find the strength to forgive—not just others, but ourselves—for the choices we regret? Muriel's journey demonstrates that even when life's storms threaten to overwhelm, faith and courage can lead us to the other side, where redemption and new beginnings await.

MURIEL A. EVANS was born in North Carolina. After college she followed her twin brother and older brother to Providence, Rhode Island where she lived for fifteen years until she married and relocated to Maryland. As a resident of Rhode Island, she worked as a Policy Analyst for the late Governor Bruce Sundlun where she served as a member of the Electoral College casting the vote for Rhode Island to elect William Jefferson Clinton.

Deciding to start a family, she switched from the political arena to the non-profit world where she has served in leadership roles as a development professional for the past eighteen years. Muriel has a Master of Science in Organizational Leadership from Nyack University, Bachelor of Science in Speech Pathology & Audiology from Shaw University, Private Investigator certificate and a certificate for Management Essentials from Harvard. She is the proud mother of Kennedy who is a reporter for NBC News in Providence.

CHAPTER 12

Crushable: Trusting God through Grief, Loss, and Change

by Marvia Sawyer

"Blessed is the man who trusts in the LORD, And whose hope is in the LORD, For he shall be like a tree planted by the waters, Which spreads out its roots by the river, And will not fear when the heat comes; But its leaf will be green, And will not be anxious in the year of drought, Nor will cease from yielding fruit."

—Jeremiah 17:7-8 (NKJV)

A few years ago, this became one of the anchor scriptures by which I aspired to live. I trusted in the Lord and was a prisoner of hope. However, when my trust and hope were put to the test, and the heat and drought season consumed me, my leaves were no longer green, and I ceased from yielding fruit. I felt like the journey to my anticipated destination was derailed or would never happen. Words like unspeakable, frightening, and devastating barely capture the weight of this experience. This is my crushing journey—a testimony of how trusting God and embracing His process transformed my pain into power.

The Crushing

The verb crush means "compress or squeeze forcefully so as to break, damage, or distort in shape."[2] Being crushable formally means "That can be crushed."[3] The words you thought you'd never hear strike like a knife, draining the lifeblood from your heart. Doubt and disbelief have now taken root, and the crushing begins.

My mind replayed my crushing journey on an endless loop, drowning out peace with relentless noise. This was a private viewing for me only. I didn't have any positive thoughts. It was impossible to concentrate, sleep, or eat. Sadness, defeat, and hopelessness hovered over me. Countless days, I woke up in tears and felt defeated. When I reflected on God's goodness, the negative thoughts were replaced with peace, hope, and healing.

At the beginning of the journey family and friends encouraged me, "You are strong, a warrior, you got this, you will feel better soon, you will get through this, and I am praying for you." I sincerely appreciated the outpour of love, vote of confidence, and prayers, but when I heard those words over and over, instead of smiling and saying thank you, sometimes, I just wanted to scream out.... "NO! I WILL NOT FEEL BETTER! I CANNOT SURVIVE THIS! STOP SAYING I AM STRONG WHEN I AM AT MY WEAKEST. CAN'T YOU SEE THIS CLOAK OF FEAR I AM WEARING THAT IS GETTING HEAVIER DAILY?" I quickly realized that they could not truly "see" or "feel" this crushing journey, for it was mine alone. No guests allowed. But wait... I am never alone, right?

---

2   www.languages.oup.com

3   www.en.wiktionary.org

Journey Alone, Yet Not Alone

I felt alone, abandoned, forgotten, despondent, and tormented. How could this be? I thought. I need a quick healing. *God, where are you?* The journey was becoming more tumultuous daily. The battlefield of my mind was riddled with landmines that were increasing with every step I took. The five stages of grief—denial, anger, bargaining, depression, and acceptance—became the rhythm of my days, shifting like a stormy-weather forecast.

"Today Marvia's weather forecast is a twenty percent chance of *denial* with fifty percent *depression* and *anger* rolling in by noon. Then ending the day with *bargaining* and hitting an all-time low of *acceptance*."

But wait! Just when I felt that God did not hear my prayers, He led me to Deuteronomy 31:8 (NKJV): "And the LORD, He is the One who goes before you. He will be with you; He will never leave you nor forsake you; do not fear or be dismayed." He reminded me of His faithfulness as a promise keeper. It was time to quiet the voices in my head and not trust my "feelings" but trust and know that God was with me on this journey. I started embracing the power and strength that God renewed in me and was ready for battle. Well, so I thought.

Don't Lose Heart

With my renewed strength, I was winning battles and managing better than before. However, at the pinnacle of my crushing journey of grief, loss, and change I folded under pressure. I experienced two deaths— one being a parent; a separation and divorce after twenty-eight years of marriage, significant changes at work—the team I led for five years was dissolved, given a new team to lead, and a new manager and business partners to quickly build relationships in another state. The hurt and pain seared my soul daily. I needed a spiritual sedative to calm me and instruct me on how to escape, navigate, or remove the pain.

The armor that I relied upon to get me through what seemed like small battles, in comparison to this "crushing," was mentally compromised and the fight in me was waning. I prayed fervently in my prayer closet. There were days I could not see past the tears to pray the scriptures. I relied on the Holy Spirit to guide me. "In the same way, the Spirit helps us in our weakness. We do not know what we ought to pray for, but the Spirit himself intercedes for us through wordless groans" (Romans 8:26 NIV). Daily, I had to declare that I would live and not die, nor lose heart, and STAND!

Knowledge is Power

As our amazing God does, He led me to watch an interview with Bishop T.D. Jakes and Pastor Steven Furtick about Bishop Jakes' book *Crushing: God Turns Pressure Into Power*. The book focuses on "God's process for growth and finding hope in life's darkest moments" (Jakes, 2019a), and the transformation in your life that takes place.

In the interview, Bishop Jakes talks about his own crushing journey and how God uses difficult, crushing experiences to prepare you for unexpected blessings. I devoured the book upon arrival, quickly gaining a better understanding of why the crushing was necessary, and that the process had to be endured for the necessary transformation.

In the book, Bishop Jakes talks about winemaking and how the process takes time to crush and transform the grapes into a fine wine. He likens winemaking to what God does to transform us and "how crushing may be necessary in order for our potential to be fulfilled." He also states, "We were created to be more than temporary fruit—we are eternal wine in the making." (Jakes, 2019a).

Bishop Jakes provided three questions to ponder. Using those questions as my benchmark, I paused to evaluate *my* crushing journey's current state, and this changed everything for me:

1. **Could it be possible that my current crushing journey is the winepress God uses to transform my grapes into His wine?** Without a doubt. This was a crushing process, and I was being transformed. The crushing revealed that there was more to my life than what my small mind planned and imagined. This meant that the crushing journey would produce His plans and purpose for my life for His glory and not mine. I heard the message loud and clear—As Romans 12:2b (NKJV) states I was being "transformed by the renewing of your [my] mind." I could see it, feel it, and embrace it happening.

2. **Could being crushed be a necessary part of the process to fulfill God's plan for my life?** At the peak of my crushing journey when I thought I could not endure anymore, He showed me that I am a survivor, and I could endure the process with the power I possessed from the pain and pressure of being crushed. I was learning to embrace and not despise the crushing journey, for I wanted to walk out God's plan for my life more than anything. He was strategically anointing me for His purpose and plan.

3. **Could you be on the precipice of victory despite walking through the valley of darkness?** Despite the pains of the crushing journey, I was already walking in victory. I found solace

in being a prisoner of hope, trusting in God and knowing that He is a promise keeper who protects and guides me and offers me a place of rest and peace, even in the crushing. "Yea, though I walk through the valley of the shadow of death, I will fear no evil; For you *are* with me; Your rod and Your staff they comfort me" (Psalm 23:4 NKJV). This confirmed what my crushing journey with God would be like. Hallelujah!

God's Plan

Amid my crushing journey, God surrounded me with six women who were traveling on a similar crushing journey. This was uncanny, unbelievable, and undeniable that God was in the midst of this. This afforded us opportunities to share our experiences and resources, pray, and offer each other support. Albeit my heart ached for these six women and their families, I was thankful that God showed us that we were not alone and how we could heal and turn our pain into power, by leaning on Him and each other. Amazing, right? God was using my life-changing, heart-wrenching, painful crushing experience to help others. I drew strength from helping others and thanked God for giving me the opportunity to make an impact during a time when I felt like I was in a drought with brown leaves, yielding no fruit, and had nothing to give.

I am crushable. My crushing journey continues today but, I am wiser and more powerful than ever before. The crushing journey increased my prayer time and deepened my relationship with God. I found myself trusting and depending on Him more. The lessons I have learned are evident in many facets of my life. I see the transformation of who I have become and continue evolving. I stand in awe at how God used the worst times in my life for my good and His glory. He transformed my pain into power. I urge you not to give up! Trust that God has a plan even amidst your pain. Try not to despise nor be distracted by the crushing. Focus on how this process is playing a part in the shaping and molding of your mind, body, and spirit; positioning you to fulfill God's plan for your life. Trust God. Trust the Process. Trust the Transformation.

> "Your crushing is not the end! It's only the beginning."
> —Bishop T.D. Jakes

> *"For we are God's masterpiece. He has created us anew in Christ Jesus, so we can do the good things he planned for us long ago."*
> —Ephesians 2:10 (NLT)

Reflections on Resilience

Marvia's testimony offers a profound lesson in perseverance, trust, and the transformative power of God. Her story reminds us that while the crushing seasons of life are painful, they are not pointless. These seasons, though devastating, are the divine press that turns ordinary fruit into extraordinary wine. In the midst of grief, loss, and change, we are invited to trust in God's process, even when His plan is unclear.

The crushing reveals not only our vulnerabilities but also our resilience. Marvia's journey underscores the importance of leaning into God's promises, even when doubt and despair seem overwhelming. As she discovered, it's through these trials that we are shaped and prepared for a greater purpose—one we may not yet see but must trust is coming. Her faithfulness in the face of pain teaches us that our darkest moments can lead to our brightest victories.

Resource

Jakes. 2019. *Crushing: God Turns Pressure Into Power*. New York: Hatchette Book Group, Inc.

MARVIA SAWYER, MBA is a manager for a Fortune 500 Company, entrepreneur, and certified Life Coach. She is the visionary founder of Being Uncommon, LLC, a life coaching, career and leadership development business. She is passionate about inspiring others to unlock their true potential by helping them to awaken their consciousness, gain clarity, and commit to executing their transformation to "be" uncommon. With her expertise and experience, she has coached and mentored countless individuals and helped them to meet and exceed their life goals. She is a member of Delta Sigma Theta Sorority, Incorporated. She is the proud mother of two daughters, Quest and Brie. Apart from her professional achievements she loves to travel, go to the theater, spend quality time with family and friends, exercise, and unwind at the beach.

Connect and Share

If you enjoyed *Uncommon Endurance,* please share this book with others who may benefit from it and leave a review on Amazon, Barnes & Noble and/or the website where you purchased it.

www.ingramcontent.com/pod-product-compliance
Lightning Source LLC
Chambersburg PA
CBHW071007120626
46546CB00003B/975

* 9 7 8 1 9 5 3 5 3 5 8 4 9 *